W0008147
MW006.79417

"Getting your way
is the gateway
to getting what
you want."

– Jeffrey Gitomer

Getting your way is something that you want all the time.

The questions you have to ask yourself are:
Why do I not always get my way?
What skills do I need to master so that
I can get my way as often as I want?

Is there a secret to getting your way?
The answer is NO! BUT, there are tons of
smart ways to get your way.

Page by page, you will discover how to
take my ideas and strategies – understand
them, apply them, become proficient at
them, and master them, so you can get
your way, and the other person, or the
other people, feel great about it.

Jeffrey Gitomer's
LITTLE GREEN BOOK
of
GETTING YOUR WAY

*How to Speak, Write, Present,
Persuade, Influence, and
Sell Your Point of View to Others*

FT Press
FINANCIAL TIMES

The Little Green Book of Getting Your Way

Copyright © 2007 by Jeffrey Gitomer. All rights reserved.

Excellent cartoons by Randy Glasbergen © 2007
www.glasbergen.com

© 2007 Pearson Education, Inc. Publishing as FT Press
Upper Saddle River, New Jersey 07458.
Vice President and Editor-in-Chief: Tim Moore.

Permission to reproduce or transmit in any form or by any means, electronic
or mechanical, including photocopying and recording, or by any information
storage and retrieval system, must be obtained in writing from the author, Jeffrey
Gitomer.

The Little Green Book of Getting Your Way is a registered trademark of
Jeffrey Gitomer.

To order additional copies of this title, contact your local bookseller or call
704/333-1112.

The author may be contacted at the following address:
BuyGitomer
310 Arlington Ave., Loft 329
Charlotte, NC 28203
Phone: 704/333-1112 Fax: 704/333-1011
E-mail: salesman@gitomer.com
Web sites: www.gitomer.com, www.trainone.com

Content and style editor: Jessica McDougall
Page designer: Mike Wolff
Cover designer: Josh Gitomer

Printed in China by RR Donnelley.

Box set edition, October 2007

Library of Congress Cataloging-in-Publication Data

Gitomer, Jeffrey H.
  Little green book of getting your way : how to speak, write, present, persuade,
influence, and sell your point of view to others / Jeffrey Gitomer.
      p. cm.
  ISBN 0-13-157607-0 (hardback : alk. paper)
  ISBN 978-0-13-157607-0
    1. Persuasion (Rhetoric) I. Title.

P301.5.P47G58 2007
303.3'42--dc22   2007000469

Can you please just do it MY WAY? Please? Pretty please?

Everyone wants it their way. Especially you. You have been trying to persuade people since you were a baby. Crying, smiling, banging your hands on the table… primitive to be sure – but effective.

Babies tend to get their way. So do little kids. Remember the aisle of the grocery store with your mom? Begging for that candy bar? *That* was persuasion. *That* was persistence. *That* was tenacity. *That* was a performance. And most of the time, you got your way.

Remember high school dating? *That* was persuasion. *That* was persistence. *That* was tenacity. *That* was a performance.

But it seems that after you got your business cards printed, some of the tenacity associated with your early persuasion skills (and persistence skills) went missing.

Fear not. You may have to call on a different set of skills (no more crying, begging, or throwing a fit), but you have the natural ability to get your way. All you have to do is uncover it, and practice it until you master it.

Getting your way takes many forms. Wanting others to see your perspective, agree with your ideas, and do what you want them to do is a skill – a science. It can be learned and mastered in a manner as to not be offensive.

Getting your way is a life skill. To master it, you may have to change your ways of thinking and interacting with others. Everything from your spoken word to your unspoken body language. Everything from what you wear to the image you project.

Presentation skills are not just for selling a product or service; presentation skills are for selling yourself – to persuade others and get your way.

> This book has the persuasion and performance answers you're looking for – whether it's sales, service, internal communications, friends, or family – and they are about to be revealed.

Look at the way others persuade you. You're asked to do things and take actions. And you do them. What better way to learn to get your way than to see yourself being persuaded, taking action as a result of it, and loving it?

The key to getting your way is to let the other person feel great after he or she has decided to see it or do it your way. In order to accomplish this, there has to be an understanding of "how" to best persuade and get your way.

Getting your way and persuasion are the same... almost.

Persuasion is the tactic you use to get your way.

– Jeffrey Gitomer

Getting your way is...

- Getting your way is the end result of your ability to persuade.

- Getting your way is the objective that you have in mind when you begin a conversation.

- Getting your way is the thought process you use when you create a presentation.

- Getting your way is the outcome of a successful sales call, negotiation, or meeting.

- Getting your way is a mindset at first and then a vision that's followed through.

- Getting your way is dependent on your ability and desire to master the elements of the process.

NOTE: Inside this book, the word *persuasion* and the phrase *getting your way* will be used interchangeably.

I am against the process of manipulation, but at some point, the tenacity and persistence you use in trying to get your way, combined with your persuasive strategies, may lead to some form of it.

My challenge to you, as you use persuasion to a point where it becomes manipulation to get your way is: keep it light, be positive, end happy.

There are 500 books written about persuasion and the manipulative elements that accompany it. This is NOT one of those books.

The contents of this book challenge you and help you in the personal development areas of thinking, planning, writing, and speaking in a compelling manner – compelling enough and passionate enough – to get others to perceive your point of view as safe and drive them to be willing, even eager, to go along with it.

This may be the first book ever to deal with the positive elements of persuasion that, when mastered, will lead you to getting your way, positively.

*"Rule #1: Always let the other guy have his way.
After you've convinced him that your way is his way!"*

Persuasion and getting your way are forms of selling...get over it

All the people who hate sales, all the people who hate salesmen are, in fact, salespeople themselves. You may be an accountant; you may be a policeman; you may be an engineer; you may be a banker. Every one of those positions involves some sort of persuasion and selling. In short, some form of getting your way.

You have meetings; you have committees; you have interactions with co-workers; you have family members; you have friends.

In all those relationships and interactions, there are times when you seek to get your way. And when you do, get this one thing loud and clear: YOU HAVE MADE A SALE.

You have sold someone else on your point of view, idea, request, or requirement – and you have done so in a manner that was compelling enough to get others to say yes, agree with you, go along with you, and give you what you want. *In other words, Jackson, you got your way.*

Throughout this book, you will see the words sale and selling. They're both forms of getting your way. And if you don't think that you employ sales tactics and sales strategies in every facet of your life, you need to change your thinking before you continue reading, or this book will do you no good.

Jeffrey Gitomer's
LITTLE GREEN BOOK
of

GETTING
YOUR
WAY

Table of Contents

Expanded Table of Contents

ELEMENT SEVEN
SALES PERSUASION PERFORMANCES

ELEMENT EIGHT
THE WRITE WAY TO GET YOUR WAY

ELEMENT NINE
PERSISTENCE

ELEMENT NINE point FIVE
ELOQUENCE

ELEMENT
1

GETTING
READY
TO GET
YOUR WAY

"Before you can get your way – you have to prepare to get your way."

While you're trying to get your way – others are perceiving and defining your words and actions

Wanting to get your way may have others define you as persistent, stubborn, hardheaded, or some other form of being tenacious. But the bottom line of other's perception of you is the way, the manner by which, you choose to try to get your way.

Throughout the process of trying to get your way, other people are receiving your message and forming an opinion of it. Based on your actions, based on your words, and even based on your looks or style of dress, others may decide, or make up their mind, before they have even heard or read your message.

You have an image of what you want and made elaborate plans; you have this huge desire to get your way, and in less than one minute – the other person (or the other people) has mentally turned you down, or worse, shut you out.

As you try to persuade, as you try to get your way – others are *perceiving*. They're perceiving a combination of who they believe you are, and the voracity of what you're trying to persuade them to do or think. *And that perception is your reality.*

Throughout this book, you will be prodded and jolted to change your ways of thinking and interacting with others. Everything from what you wear, to what you say, to the way you say it, to what your body says while your saying it. You'll be asked to do things, say things, try things, think about things, and take action.

Why not learn more ways of getting others to see it your way? There's no better way to learn persuasion than to see yourself being persuaded, taking action as a result of it, and loving it.

"Next time, instead of trying to persuade the car to stop, why don't you just wait for the light to change."

If you agree with me so far, I have done my job to get you to turn the page...

Persuasion is the process... getting your way is the outcome

The prime strategy for getting your way is implementing a persuasion process that leads to a positive outcome.

The two-word secret of how to be persuasive and how to implement persuasion strategies is *manipulation free*. Manipulated persuasion is short lived. True persuasion exists when it lasts beyond the moment.

Persuasion is a science. You can learn to persuade. You can learn the best ways to persuade in each given situation of your business life, your sales life, and your personal life.

Persuasion is an art. Never crossing the line to "pushy." It's showing reserve and poise. In short – being cool.

Persuasion is excellent questioning skills beyond excellent communication skills. It's getting the other person to clarify what you want in their mind. Rather than tell them "This is why that happened..." ask "Why do you think this happened" or "What made this happen?" It's a subtle but powerful difference.

Persuasion is compromise. Often there is some give and take in order to get to your way.

Persuasion is asking questions that clarify the situation. Asking for elaboration, understanding, and "why" will lead you to harmony. That harmony will permit open-minded dialog.

Persuasion is excellent listening skills. Listening is one of the most difficult elements of persuasion because it requires patience. The two-word secret of patience and listening is *not* "shut up." It's "take notes." Taking notes shows respect and eliminates miscommunication.

Persuasion is getting the other guy to convince himself. If you question, listen, write it down, and question again for clarification, your answers and your point of view will become obvious.

Persuasion is preparation. Gathering the right information. Creating the right questions. Uncovering the right hot buttons – and acting on them.

Persuasion is victory. Persuasion is the science by which you get your way. It's not just getting your way; it's persuading with harmony and getting everyone to agree. It's you getting your way without the other guy feeling like he or she "lost."

Persuasion is reading this book more than once. And putting the elements into action.

"I did it my way!" is *not* the way that song should have ended. If Frank or Elvis were masters of persuasion, they would have sung: "I did it my way, and everyone agreed with me!"

Thinking you can is 50%

1

If you want to be convincing...
If you want to persuade others to your way of thinking...
If you want to get your way...

Then the first person you have to persuade is *yourself.*

If you're not convinced, how can you convince others? If you're not convinced, what do you think the conviction behind your words will be? Two-word answer: Not very.

Have you ever seen someone on television delivering one of those infomercials about a pill or an exercise machine? Have you ever picked up the phone and purchased? Sure you have; everyone has. The salesperson was convincing enough and persuasive enough to get their way.

They were so convincing, they were so persuasive, that they got you to take out your credit card and spend money. But before they were able to get one dime out of you, they had to spend thousands (maybe hundreds of thousands) getting ready, preparing their product, and preparing their message.

Why did you buy it? Well, one of the reasons is that you believed their message. You were convinced, or persuaded, that whatever it was that they were selling would benefit you. And you bought.

You've even purchased non-necessity infomercial items like kitchen appliances, tools, and other things you thought would make your life easier.

"I don't know how he does it, but that guy always makes me feel like I'm the center of the universe!"

NOTE WELL: Before these people could ever convince you, they had to convince themselves. They had to believe in it before they could get you to believe in it.

But there's a deeper secret than thinking you can. Thinking you can is at the surface level. If you want the deeper secret of "thinking you can," keep reading.

The secret of self-belief

If I teach you everything I know about persuasion and getting your way, and if you go out and read 10 other books on the subject and become an expert, you will *never* be able to persuade anyone else or get your way, unless you believe in yourself first.

Self-belief is a common thread that runs through all of my books and all of my writing. There's a reason: Self-belief is at the core, the very fulcrum point, of your ability to succeed at anything – not just getting your way.

If your self-belief is not strong enough to evoke and emote your passion, then others will not catch it, nor be convinced or persuaded that your idea, or your product, or your way, is best for them.

I began studying and understanding self-belief in 1972 when I was involved in network marketing (now called direct selling). Someone told me that in order for me to succeed, I had to become "A product of the product."

At first I didn't understand what was meant by *becoming a product of the product.*

Turns out I had to *believe in it* before I could convince others to become part of it.

And the best way to build that belief was to use the product I was selling myself. If I wasn't using it, how could I sell it?

If you go to a car dealership and the salesperson isn't driving the same kind of car that he's selling, why should you even consider buying it? He doesn't believe in it enough to own it.

If you ask yourself "How much do I believe in what I'm doing?" the answer will reveal your probability of persuading others, and getting your way.

These are the fundamental beliefs necessary for you to achieve success, persuade others, and get your way:

- **Believe in yourself.**
- **Believe in what you're doing.**
- **Believe in your product.**
- **Believe in your company.**

And there's one more secret…

You have to believe that by persuading the other person you are helping them – and that after you have persuaded them, they will benefit.

– Jeffrey Gitomer

The secret of attitude

The glue of self-belief and thinking you can is based in your attitude – the way you dedicate yourself to the way you think.

If you don't own my *Little Gold Book of YES! Attitude* now would be a great time to go out and make that small investment. You will learn that attitude is not just a feeling or an expression – it's a science. You teach yourself and you dedicate yourself to positive thinking, reacting, and living.

Your positive thoughts are the ones that build every aspect of your self-belief. Your positive thoughts are the basis for your personal persuasion – your ability to tell yourself that you can do it, that you will find a way to make it happen, and that the outcome will be a positive one.

> Getting your way is not simply a matter of being compelling; it's a matter of being positively compelling.

Of course there are exceptions to any process. And when negative things occur that cause actions – an illness, a heart attack, even a death – those events may persuade you to change your feeling or change your ways. But in your mind, you still have to discover "What good will come of this?" or "How can I make this happen the best way?" or "How can I make the best of this situation?"

Even when persuasion is negative, you still have to hope for a positive outcome, search for a positive outcome, and believe that a positive outcome is possible.

The opposite of those "possible" thoughts is the easy way out: resigning yourself to the situation, or just giving up.

Positive attitude, when combined with positive thinking and positive self-belief, will provide the foundation necessary for you:

- **To become passionate about what you do and what you want.**
- **To be able to convince others.**
- **To be able to persuade others.**
- **To be able to get others to see your way.**

The elements in the rest of this book will teach you the strategies and methods of getting your way, but you must be the essence of self-belief and *YES!*Attitude in order to transfer your message.

You may want to read these first 24 pages again. They are the basis, and provide the core personal values upon which you will be able to persuade others and get your way.

Thinking and believing are the building blocks of your passion and conviction. Add your attitude into the mix, and you have the cement and steel to build a rock-solid, consistent, mental foundation.

ELEMENT

2

THE FUNDAMENTALS OF GETTING YOUR WAY

"I've always been able to get my way. Why do I need the fundamentals?"

"There's a big difference between getting your way and being manipulative."

The squeaky wheel gets its way

You've heard the expression "the squeaky wheel gets the oil." The wheel is telling you, "Hey, I need oil." But you're annoyed at the sound of the squeak, so you give it oil to make the noise go away.

Clearly this is not the only method of getting your way, but it's an easy example for you to begin to understand the process.

If you want to get your way, you have to learn how to squeak. I'll define it later on as *how to SPEAK*, but you get the idea.

Getting your way in life has to do with thinking you'll get your way, believing you'll get your way, making a game plan for getting your way, perfecting your writing and presentation skills for getting your way, executing your game plan for getting your way, modifying your game plan on the fly to get your way, and persisting in all of these elements until you succeed at getting your way.

NOTE: You will not get your way all the time. BUT, by polishing your skills, deepening your belief, and developing a passion for what you want – you *will* get your way more often.

Understanding how to persuade and get your way

As I said in the beginning, *everybody wants to get their way*. It's one of the unwritten laws of the universe.

You've been working at it since you were an infant. Your method of persuading was crying. You had no other way of communicating that you wanted a clean diaper, or you were hungry, or you were tired. It worked.

As you grew up, oftentimes your emotional plea would go over the edge. As you progressed, you were able to combine words with emotion. In childrearing they call it a tantrum, or pitching a fit. And much of the time it worked. Negative, but it worked.

Your growing up experiences have a lot to do with your ability to persuade others and get your way. So does your personality.

The outgoing, friendly, aggressive, assertive ones tend to have more "luck" than the meek.

Fast forward to getting your business card printed. You're still seeking to get your way. Add that to the fact that you may have learned manipulation techniques from your experiences, or may *need* to get your way, not just want to get your way.

Some people's skills for persuasive manipulation are learned from books and teachers, others are self-taught by trial and error. But you currently have and use a way, or ways, of convincing and persuading others.

The fundamentals that follow will help you understand why you do it your way and how you might want to change in order to improve your existing results.

TO GET YOUR WAY, YOU HAVE TO BE ABLE TO CONVINCE OTHERS.

Convincing others has to do with your own conviction (see pages 19-24) coupled with your ability to articulate a believable message.

Your message has to make sense, and your message has to contain a "what's in it for me" element that allows the other person to feel valued and be persuaded.

The principles of convincing others are personal conviction, being believable, telling the truth, and providing value.

TO GET YOUR WAY, YOU HAVE TO BE ABLE TO INFLUENCE OTHERS.

You've heard and read the phrase, "He's a very influential person." You can look at a million dictionary definitions, but the reality is that influential person is able to make you think about what you're doing and possibly make changes or improvements to it.

Their manner of influence is powerful enough to make you part with your money, change your mind, and change your ways.

BUT HERE'S A SECRET: Being a person of influence means that you have *reputation*, *character*, *credibility*, and *stature* enough that people will take your message seriously. Reputation, character, credibility, and stature come from your track record and your success record combined with your perceived expertise.

People of influence also have actual or personal power. You've heard it referred to as, "The power to influence."

Your ability to influence others is often based on their perception of (and belief in) you. You may be influential in some circles and not in others. The better your reputation is, the more likely it is that you are able to influence others.

The principles of influencing others are character, credibility, stature, history of success, and reputation.

TO GET YOUR WAY, YOU HAVE TO POSSESS PERSUASIVE PRESENTATION SKILLS.

An integral part of your ability to influence and convince others is your ability to communicate your message.

There are thousands of Toastmasters clubs and equally thousands of speech coaches and courses that you can take on presentation skills, yet it's the least studied and certainly the least mastered skill in the science of persuasion and the art of getting your way.

> If I had a dollar for every corporate leader, from CEOs to branch managers, who had lousy presentation skills, I'd be a multi-billionaire.

This book is drenched in presentation skills. You will learn how to harness the power of persuasion by enhancing, and ultimately mastering, your ability to present, persuade, and convince others to see your point of view in an engaging and positive way.

The principles of persuasive presentation skills are passion, convinceability, excellence of message delivery, the ability to create examples that are easily understood, and being able to transfer your message in a way that others agree with you and are willing to take action based on that agreement.

TO GET YOUR WAY, YOU HAVE TO BE A PERSUASIVE STORYTELLER.

Everyone loves a good story. Books are sold by the billions, and their owners eagerly read someone else's story in long or short form.

Short stories have always been my favorite. They get to the heart of the situation right away, and the endings are often a surprise – something you weren't expecting. There's also the satisfaction that the story is over right away – you get to know how it turns out in less than one day, maybe even less than one hour.

2

Stories contain drama. Drama (or should I say "other people's drama") seems to be at the root of what drives the American population to spend their time. Personally, I would rather write a story, or tell a story, than listen to or watch someone else's drama. The exception is listening to someone I respect or admire because I might learn something new from their story.

What's your story?

Think about how you tell a story. Oftentimes you will hear someone say "I'm not very good at telling stories" or "I'm not very good at telling jokes." Why would you write yourself a death sentence before you even begin? Why wouldn't you say something like, "I am trying to get better at telling stories. Listen to this one."

That one little change in your personal mental structure will automatically make you a better storyteller.

Stories convey a message in metaphor format, or by telling of a similar situation. These two elements are not only convincing, but they will often make the listener think of their own story, thereby convincing themselves. This, by the way, is the most powerful element of persuasion.

The principles of persuasive storytelling are having a meaningful message, making the story germane to what's being discussed, being able to tell it in a convincing manner, and combining your theatrical skills with your presentation skills to add the element of performance to the presentation of your story.

2

TO GET YOUR WAY, YOU HAVE TO POSSESS PERSUASIVE WRITING SKILLS.

I've written before, that "writing leads to wealth." Writing is also the basis of creating your own wealth of knowledge. The more you write, the better you become at clarifying your own thoughts. And the more you edit your writing, or have others edit it for you, the more clear it will become to those who read it. In the science of persuasion and the art of getting your way, writing plays an integral role – whether it's a letter, a proposal, an e-mail, or a description of what is being offered.

The best example is eBay. If you look at some of the elaborate descriptions offered by sellers, it can often convince you to bid, or even "Buy it Now." eBay Is creating an entire new generation of writers (sellers) looking to persuade others (buyers) to bid on or buy their wares.

So powerful is this eBay concept that courses are now being offered such as "How to Sell on eBay" or "How to Make Money on eBay." Subliminally, what they're saying is "How to write a persuasive description so that others will want to own what you're selling on eBay."

But writing has a much broader width and depth. eBay is just one small example of how powerful writing can be.

Before Lincoln delivered The Gettysburg Address, he handwrote it on the back of an envelope. Before song lyrics can be sung, they're written. It's the same with Broadway shows and screenplays for movies. Think about the last compelling sermon that you heard in your chosen place of worship. I guarantee it was prewritten, possibly even pre-rehearsed.

I've been writing professionally since 1992. (Writing professionally means being paid for your writing.) I force myself to become better each time I write something. I try to make my concepts more clear, I try to make my ideas more convincing, and I try to make the strategy and the methods that I suggest be compelling enough that others will adopt them and adapt them to their style and their personality.

I measure my value as a persuasive writer by the number of people who buy my books, by how long my books are able to stay on the market, and by how many cards and e-mails I receive – thanking me, and telling me that my ideas have been implemented, and they're working.

The principles of persuasive writing are clarity, creativity, voice, and the ability to inject humor to make the reader smile and want to continue.

GETTING YOUR WAY DEPENDS ON YOUR ABILITY TO TRANSFER A CONCEPT OR A MESSAGE.

A transferable concept is as powerful an element of getting your way as exists. It may be *the* most powerful element, but I'll let you decide. To me, it is.

2

Every one of the principles that I have described in this section can only be successful in persuading others if the message, the ideas, the presentation, the story, or the writings are *transferable*.

To understand a transferable concept requires that you know the process by which one occurs. You speak to a person, or you speak to an audience, or you write an article, and the person listening or reading to themselves says, *"I get it. I think I can do it. I'm willing to try it."*

In other words, the recipient of your message understands it, feels comfortable with it, and believes in it enough to take an action.

The good news is transferable concepts are easy to achieve once you understand what they are. And the best part about transferable concepts is that they work in a powerful way.

Not only do you convince others, not only do you persuade others, but you also get them to convince and persuade themselves to take an action on your behalf – or what they perceive to be in *their* best interest, that would also be in *your* best interest.

Even though transferable concepts may be new to you, there's nothing foreign or complex about them. The ability to transfer a message is a skill that you can easily acquire, put into practice immediately after you learn it, and eventually master.

The principles of transferable concepts are your ability to convey a message or messages that other people like, believe, and are confident they can do in a beneficial way.

TAKE ACTION: Now that you understand the fundamentals of getting your way, you can begin to use them, practice them, and master them in a way that will benefit everyone else and, of course, you.

"I love this book. It's all about me!"

Getting your way is not just about you. Sometimes getting your way means letting the other person have it their way as well.

– Jeffrey Gitomer

The science of compromise

I used to watch my father negotiate. He was a master at getting his way. After the deal was done, he would remind me, "Son, never offer anything you wouldn't be glad to accept yourself." I thought that was a pretty good strategy. It would certainly make you think before you tried to take advantage of someone.

When both people want it their way, and their ways are different, something has to give. *Compromise* is a good way to think of it because it involves both give and take. It's a form of *this for that*, or a form of *settling*.

"Heads, we do it my way.
Tails, we do it my other way!"

The first key to compromise is knowing where you're willing to settle. And second is getting to the middle ground of the compromise process by asking questions of the other person – rather than begging, pleading, or trying too hard to persuade.

Questioning also leads to *understanding*. "Mr. Jones, if we did it my way, what would happen? How would this negatively affect you?" Once you understand how the other person may be negatively affected, then you can understand how to compromise or, better stated, what you're willing to give up in exchange for their partial happiness.

Where do you draw the line at compromise? And how far are you willing to draw that line to get your way?

Compromise usually means no one gets everything they wanted. The key to making a good compromise is fairness. Are you okay with the outcome? Is the other person okay with the outcome?

While compromise is a science, it's one without a formula. The elements that must be present have already been discussed. Know what you're willing to give up, and ask questions to find out the other person's needs, feelings, and passions.

And, like any other form of persuasion or getting your way, you have to look at the long-term outcome and measure its value or consequence against what you're trying to achieve. That will not only help you in compromise, it will also help you in life.

ELEMENT
3

THE FUNDAMENTALS OF PERSUASION AND PERSONAL POWER

"I lick their face."

"I purr and jump in their lap."

"I'm not good at licking and purring. Maybe I need to learn the fundamentals."

Proper persuasion to get your way

If the key to getting your way is to let the other person feel great after he or she has decided to see it or do it your way, then there has to be an understanding of "how" to best persuade them.

Here are the 8.5 key elements that make up your ability to persuade others and get your way:

1. Explaining what, why, and how. People start out skeptical. They want to know: What is this? Why will this work? Why do you want me to do this? Why are you asking me? What are you trying to accomplish? What will this mean to me? How will this affect me? How do I win? Your ability to *plausibly explain* goes a long way toward getting your way.

2. Explaining what's in it for them. People are more likely to be persuaded if they see how they win as a result of following your lead or seeing it your way.

3. Your sincerity. Your conviction is part of their buy-in. False sincerity eventually shows. And smells.

4. Your believability. Are you making statements that others can relate to? That others find conceivable? Conceivable leads to believable.

5. Your questioning skills. This is one of the major keys to persuasion and getting your way. Not telling – asking. Are you asking questions that relate to the other person? Questions about them, that make them stop and think, and respond in terms of you? Powerful persuasion starts with powerful questions. Ask their opinion. Solicit their expertise. Ask about their experience.

6. Your communication skills. How would you rate your communication skills? *Eh, not too fast there, Plato.* Have you ever seen yourself present on video? Until you do, you have *no idea* how good you are, or are not.

7. Your visionary (storytelling) skills. Can you paint the picture so clearly and vividly that they can see the rain and feel the sunshine? Facts and figures are forgotten, stories are retold.

8. Your reputation precedes you. Reputation is so powerful, it can make getting your way an automatic yes if yours is exceptional, or an automatic no if yours is "iffy."

8.5 Your history of success. The more you have won in the past not only dictates your present demeanor, it also dictates the demeanor towards you of those you are trying to persuade. If you have been a winner, you can project winning. This becomes evident and transferable as you seek to persuade others and get your way.

NOTE: No one single item from this list will complete the process. The more you master each of them, the more persuasive you'll become, and the more you will get your way.

The power of persuasion

Think about how many times in your life other people have persuaded you to do it their way.

Think about how many times in your life you have been successful in persuading others to do it your way.

What made the difference? Did the people who persuaded you have greater passion, greater skill, or greater understanding of the persuasion process? Maybe they just exerted their authority – like a parent or a boss – and you did it their way, but you grumbled the whole time.

3

Regardless of who wins in the persuasion process, the underlying element is that the winner is a more powerful persuader than the loser.

I can teach you all about persuasion, but there's a self-discipline that goes with it that will determine your ability to harness the power of the information you're reading.

I believe, and have stated, that the essence of harnessing the power of persuasion is developing a strong belief system – not just one part of the belief system, the entire belief system – and to practice by doing.

Your report card will not simply be winning or getting your way. Your report card will be the reputation that you develop as a result of persuading others. What will they say about you behind your back after they have been persuaded?

The better you become at persuasion, combined with a great reputation, indicates that you have begun to harness the power that persuasion offers.

You won't harness the power of persuasion in a day. But you can harness the power of persuasion day by day.

3

"If you would work on your powers of persuasion, you wouldn't need the collar and leash!"

The essence of persuasion and personal power

As fast as you can, go get a video copy of Martin Luther King, Jr.'s "I Have a Dream" speech. Then get a copy of John F. Kennedy's inauguration address. These are two of the best examples of public presentation persuasion.

I hope you have seen Martin Luther King, Jr.'s epic talk (delivered at the foot of the Lincoln Memorial to more than 500,000 people). It's known as the "I have a dream" speech. It's less that 20 minutes long, but its impact will last for hundreds of years.

3

Not unlike Lincoln's Gettysburg Address, Martin Luther King, Jr., talked about what was, what is, and what could be. King, Jr.'s words were not only perfectly chosen, they were also delivered with eloquence and passion – the likes of which I have never seen.

I own the speech on video and audio. And personally, I have never listened to it without becoming extremely emotional – often crying. King, Jr. does not utter the phrase, "I have a dream," until almost the end of the talk, and he challenges 500,000 people to follow his dream. And they do.

John F. Kennedy's speech was full of challenges. He talked about the opportunities that Americans (and America) have.

He ended his speech with the most significant challenge ever delivered in an inaugural address, "Ask not what your country can do for you. Ask what you can do for your country."

That address was in January of 1961, and it is equally as relevant today as it was then. His speech was not only classic, it was timeless.

I'm not challenging you to run for office or create a civil rights movement. But I am challenging you that if you want to use and harness the power of persuasion, start by studying the powerful, persuasive presentations of others. They will not only inspire you, but they will also create a benchmark for what you can achieve, or what you can aspire to, in your own circle of influence.

Do you have a dream? If you do, make certain you have the passion to share it with others in a way that they can help you achieve it.

> "The ultimate measure of a man is not where he stands in moments of comfort and convenience, but where he stands at times of challenge and controversy."
>
> – Martin Luther King, Jr. (1929-1968)

> "Efforts and courage are not enough without purpose and direction."
>
> – John F. Kennedy (1917-1963)

Your power is useless unless you harness it.

– Jeffrey Gitomer

Understanding the power of engagement

When I discovered that the secret of selling was engagement, I began to study what made engagement happen.

I tell my audiences, "When a customer or prospect says, 'I am not interested,' what it means is that you are not interesting. The prospective customer will never say, 'You are not interest*ing*.' He or she will take the blame themselves and say, 'I am not interest*ed*.'"

"I'm not interested" is a symptom. The problem is you've failed to engage the other person in a way that they were willing to have some dialog with you – or that they perceived some value or difference in you, versus the other people that they have met with.

Engagement takes place when the right questions are asked – questions about the other person that make them stop and think, consider new information, and respond in terms of you.

Engagement is so powerful that you cannot carry on conversations without it, you cannot have a social life without it, you cannot make sales without it, you cannot climb the corporate ladder without it, and your ability to communicate even the most simple of challenges or ideas will be lost.

3

Like persuasion and presentation, engagement is an opportunity, an opportunity that will never be harnessed if your prime objective is to engage people about *you* before you try to engage people about *them*.

> "You can make more friends in two months by becoming interested in other people, than you can in two years by trying to get other people interested in you."
>
> – Dale Carnegie

> "If the customer says they're not interested, it means you're not interesting."
>
> – Jeffrey Gitomer

Engagement is the glue of persuasion. Engagement is the glue of presentation. You can persuade all you want, you can present all you want – but if you can't engage, you won't get your way.

ELEMENT

4

THE ESSENTIALS OF GETTING YOUR WAY

"When I give my 30-second personal commercial, why does everyone run to the refrigerator to grab something to eat?"

"It's their polite way of being impolite."

Professional development of a presenter

1. GET READY. Your content, your humor, your speed of delivery, your tone, your gestures, your passion, your familiarity, your story, your conciseness, and your punch.

CLUE: Know the audience, pre-question some of the attendees, or die.

2. ASK YOURSELF 8.5 QUESTIONS.

1. What's my time limit?
2. Is this the most compelling message I can create?
3. What's the point I am trying to make?
4. Am I engaging?
5. What will persuade the audience?
6. Am I clear? Is my message clear?
7. Is my delivery the best it can be?
8. What do I want the audience to do when I'm done?
8.5 What do I want the audience to say to me (or about me) when I am done?

CLUE: The answers to these questions will tighten your talk and make it great. Your objective is to deliver the message in such a way that the audience is compelled to act.

3. PRACTICE IN FRONT OF PEOPLE WHO ARE NOT AFRAID TO EVALUATE YOU.

4. RECORD A PRACTICE SESSION. If you listen to the recording and say to yourself *this sucks* – that's what your audience will think. It's you – fix it.

5. LISTEN TO YOUR RECORDING AS OFTEN AS YOU CAN STAND IT. Memorize and know where you need emphasis. Know what sounds stupid – cut that out. Re-record it.

6. PRACTICE IT AS THOUGH YOU WERE GIVING IT. Rehearse for real every time.

7. IF YOUR FAMILY OR FRIENDS THINK YOU'RE NUTS, YOU'RE ON THE RIGHT TRACK.

8. APPOINT AN EVALUATOR BEFORE YOU START EACH TALK.

9. VIDEOTAPE THE ACTUAL SESSION.

9.5 WATCH THE TAPE TWICE. Make a list of "never do that again" items and carry it with you for three years.

I've just given you the elements of what you need to create and deliver a memorable presentation. On the next page, I'm going to give you a list of strategies to implement and execute that will make your presentation compelling.

But be aware that simply reading the list is not enough. You have to put each item from the list into action. And then slowly over time you will evolve into an excellent presenter.

Here are 11.5 guidelines to a compelling presentation:

1. **Relax.** It's a speech, not a trial.

2. **The more prepared you are, the less nervous you will be.**

3. **Get the audience to like you.** As soon as possible.

4. **Don't thank anyone for anything at the beginning of your talk.** Start as though you were in the middle of your talk and make an engaging point as fast as you can.

5. **If you're somewhat funny, you have a better chance of connecting.** Funny engages.

6. **They don't care about you.** They care about them. Speak about them.

7. **Material beats style.** Material beats dress.

8. **Style and dress enhance great material.**

9. **Use transferable concepts.** They engage.

10. **Be one notch better than anyone in the audience.** But present on their level.

11. **Have several signature words, phrases, and gestures.** They engage.

11.5 **Know the audience.** Know their business and their nuances before you say a word.

HERE'S THE SECRET: The more you speak and the better you become, the more you will get your way.

The first few minutes that you talk to someone, they decide if they like you or not.

The more you talk about, and ask about, them, the more they will like you.

– Jeffrey Gitomer

Look good, act better, persuade best, and get your way

When you're in the heat of presenting, the way you look and act can increase (or take away from) your ability to engage and your ability to persuade.

Every item in the list below is something you already know how to do, or have been told to do. The problem is you may not be doing it. Do this exercise as a self-assessment. Then have a friend or co-worker (or your boss, if you dare) fill out the same test, rating you. Compare answers.

Circle the number on the right that comes closest to your present situation or skill level.

1=Never, 2=Rarely, 3=Sometimes, 4=Frequently, 5=All the time

4

☐ I stand up straight. 1 2 3 4 5

☐ I have clear, bright eyes, not red, bleary, tired eyes. 1 2 3 4 5

☐ My talking pace is perfect. 1 2 3 4 5

☐ I make good eye contact that breeds and shows confidence. 1 2 3 4 5

☐ If I smoke, I don't smell like a cigarette.   **1   2   3   4   5**

☐ I wear appropriate clothing.   **1   2   3   4   5**

☐ I look crisp. My clothes are ironed.   **1   2   3   4   5**

☐ I look professional — as good as the people I am speaking to, or better.   **1   2   3   4   5**

☐ I have first-class accessories (briefcase, bag, pens).   **1   2   3   4   5**

☐ I have everything prepared and in order before I begin.   **1   2   3   4   5**

☐ I am relaxed.   **1   2   3   4   5**

☐ I wear a smile.   **1   2   3   4   5**

If any 1s, 2s, or 3s were circled, check the box next to the left of the statement and get better. If you have no 1s, 2s, or 3s, work on your 4s. If you have all 5s, you must be the best and most wealthiest presenter in the world. I need a big bank loan. Please call me to arrange terms.

Let someone else take this test and rate you. In presenting, it doesn't matter how you see yourself as much as it matters how others see you.

Harmonizing NOT manipulating

Many people confuse persuasion with manipulation, or pressure. Big mistake.

In the early days of selling, sales often had a first name. "High-pressure." The telemarketing room was referred to as a "boiler room." But the reality is, persuasion has to be coupled with the phrase *long term*.

At the end of persuasion, there's an *outcome*. You've convinced someone to do it your way, and something will happen as a result of it.

A long-term relationship will often depend on the outcome of what has been persuaded.

If you're trying to force someone, or sell someone, your motive may not be long term. Short-term sales are often evident by the language and the tactics of the salesperson. They use what are called sales techniques. But really, it's manipulation or, to take it deeper, mental manipulation. You can probably relate it to the phrase "playing with your emotions" or "pushy salespeople."

The good side of persuasion is *harmonizing*. This means, either by logic or emotion, you have persuaded one person or a group of people to see it your way, do it your way, buy into it, or buy.

Persuasion comes in all forms. It can be as light as wanting something from your parents, wanting a date, convincing your partner to see it your way instead of his, controlling the remote, going to a ball game versus going shopping, or it can get heavier – which car, which house, which college, even which spouse.

Every one of those decisions contains elements of persuasion, even if the person you're persuading is yourself.

The more harmony you have, the less remorse you're likely to have a short time later. Some people refer to it as "second guessing" or "buyer's remorse." I prefer to call it "reality" or "reality setting in." The reality of money. The reality of re-evaluating feelings. Or the reality of a judgment that you made.

There is a secret about deciding emotionally and regretting it. The secret is *move on*. Dwelling on what went wrong will never lead you to what is right. If something doesn't go right in the persuasion process, learn from it – don't moan about it or regret it.

Turning your personal commercial into getting your way

When you're networking, or you go to a business meeting, you're on the lookout for contacts and prospects.

Your personal commercial (also known as an elevator speech or cocktail commercial) is an opportunity to provide information that creates interest and response from the people you're networking with.

It's the prelude and the gateway to making a connection, making a sale, and getting your way.

How effective is your commercial? *Do you even have one?*

Your objective is to have thirty seconds of information. That states who you are and what company you represent, and creatively tells what you do.

After you say a little – ask a lot. Ask one (or a series of) power question that engages. Make a power statement that tells how you can help others. And end with why the prospect should act now.

The information you gain from your power questions will allow you to formulate an impact response to show that you can help. The questions must be open-ended questions, questions that get the prospect thinking and talking, not just saying yes or no.

There is no reason to tell a prospect how you can help until you have uncovered what kind of help they need.

The power question is the most critical part of the process because it qualifies the prospect, sets up your impact (power) response, and makes the prospect think.

When formulating your power questions for your commercial, ask yourself these five questions:

1. **What information do I want to get as a result of asking this question?**

2. **Can I qualify my prospect as a result of the question?**

3. **Does it take more than one question to find out the information I need?**

4. **Do my questions make the prospect think?**

5. **Can I ask a question that separates me from my competitor?**

Here are some lead-ins to power questions that will expose areas of need:

- What do you look for...
- What have you found...
- How do you propose...
- What has been your experience...
- How have you successfully used...
- How do you determine...
- Why is that a deciding factor...
- What makes you choose...
- What do you like about...
- What is one thing you would improve about...
- What would you change about...
  (Do not say "What don't you like about...")
- Are there other factors...
- What does your competitor do about...
- How do your customers react to...
- How are you currently...
- What are you doing to keep...
- How often do you contact...
- What are you doing to ensure...

You should have a list of 25 power questions that make the prospect stop and think and give you the information you need to strike.

The closure of your 30-second commercial should be a call to action – a closing line, statement, or question that ensures another contact.

Here's an example of a personal commerical:

Let's say you're out with a customer networking at her trade association meeting and she introduces you to a prospect. The prospect says, "What do you do?" If you're in the temporary staffing industry and you say, "I'm in the temporary staffing industry," you should be fired.

Your reply should be, "I provide quality emergency and temporary employees to businesses like yours so that when one of your employees is sick, absent, or on vacation, there is no loss of productivity or reduction of service to your customers." *Deliver a line like that, and the person you're speaking with can't help but be impressed.*

Now that you have the prospect's attention, ask your power questions to find out how qualified the person is.

"How many employees do you have?" you ask. "Do you give them one week or two weeks of vacation?" "How do you ensure that the level of service to your customers isn't reduced during those vacation times?"

Continue to ask more follow-up questions until you get the information you need.

After your power questions, insert your power statement (how you help) and a reason why the prospect should act now.

"I specialize in smart, capable people. Not temporary help. When your people are on vacation, or out sick, I know you can't afford low morale or a reduction in service. Here's what I propose: (This is your call to action statement and the reason your prospect should act now.) Let's meet for breakfast and discuss your last few employee absences. We'll talk about how they were handled and discuss the next few upcoming absences. If I think I can help you, I'll tell you. And if I don't think I can help you, I'll tell you that, too. Is that fair enough?"

Use this example to help you write your own personal commercial. After you write it, rehearse it. Then, go try it out and adjust it for the real world.

Then, practice it (more than 25 times in real situations) until you own it.

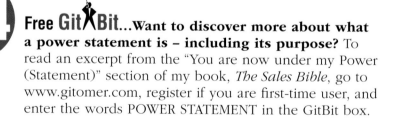

4 Free Git✗Bit...**Want to discover more about what a power statement is – including its purpose?** To read an excerpt from the "You are now under my Power (Statement)" section of my book, *The Sales Bible*, go to www.gitomer.com, register if you are first-time user, and enter the words POWER STATEMENT in the GitBit box.

Your personal commercial worksheet

INSTRUCTIONS: Fill out this two-page form. Read it from top to bottom. Add a few personal pronouns. Time it. Practice it. Study it. And voilá!

My name: _____

My company name: _____

What I do: _____

_____

_____

_____

"Before we begin our meeting, let's swap contact lenses. It might help us see things from each other's point of view!"

My power questions: _____

_____

_____

_____

_____

My power statement: _____

_____

_____

_____

_____

How can I help: _____

_____

_____

_____

_____

4

Why should the prospect act now: _____

_____

_____

_____

_____

Slide show stupidity: That's not you at the laptop, or is it?

In a hotel lobby, I passed a seller and a buyer involved in a sales presentation. The seller was deeply engrossed in "making the sale." He was intensely looking at his laptop computer as he methodically clicked through his PowerPoint presentation.

The thing that struck me was that the prospective buyer was not paying attention. Actually, he seemed to be staring off into space, completely detached from the presentation.

Noticing this, I went over to these two strangers and said to the seller, "What are you doing? This guy's not paying attention to you."

Then, I turned to the prospect and said, "Are you buying or not?" The prospect, somewhat startled, said, "Yeah, I am."

I said, "Great! Finish this transaction right this minute." Then, I walked away grinning.

This encounter reminded me of the old sales joke: "Don't buy yet. I'm not finished with my presentation." Now, although this scenario is amusing, if you use PowerPoint during a sales presentation, you – yes, you – have been in the same situation.

Most PowerPoint presentations that I see are somewhere between boring and pathetic. The object of a presentation is to present a compelling and audience-oriented message that's transferable. The object of PowerPoint is to reinforce the message of the presenter.

To create a PowerPoint presentation that is engaging and compelling, this list includes the 15.5 elements to look for, look out for, include, and exclude:

1. Don't even think about using stupid clip art that any 12-year-old could find. It makes you look like a rank amateur. Use your own clip art or photos, or use none.

2. Add an unexpected, personal, FUNNY photograph.

3. Make a verbal point and reinforce it with a slide, not the other way around.

4. Don't EVER say, "This one's a little hard to read." Slides are free. Make two of them.

5. Don't have your slides spin around or have moving text. Total waste of time.

6. Don't put more than one point on a slide.

7. Count the laughs. At least one for every five slides. (If there's at least one laugh every five slides, you can count on one other thing: money.)

8. Use a white background. The fancy ones are distracting and serve no purpose.

9. Use the font IMPACT. Set the master screen for 44pt and shadow the type.

10. Emphasize words by blowing them up a few point sizes. Make them a different color. I use red.

11. If you're laboring over one slide that you are trying to "make work," delete it. It was probably a weak point.

12. Use slides that tell a story rather than relate a fact. Stories are the most powerful part of the sale. Here's the rule: Facts and figures are forgotten, stories are remembered and retold.

*"My PowerPoint presentation went so well,
I had it made into a tattoo!"*

13. Are your slides engaging? There are two kinds of slides: engaging and distracting. Review each slide and ask yourself, "How engaging is this slide?" If it's not engaging, why are you using it?

14. Are your slides asking questions or making statements? Questions will promote conversation. Your PowerPoint presentation should engage by asking questions and promoting dialog.

15. How many of the claims that you make in your presentation, by PowerPoint or verbally, are backed up with proof? Which brings me to my final point...

15.5. Incorporate video testimonial clips throughout your slide presentation to back up and prove that your claims are real and transferable. Real, transferable, and acceptable to the audience.

By now, you're probably totally disheartened about your PowerPoint presentation because I've exposed it for the powerless "point" it is. But take heart. Your competition's slide presentation is equally pathetic.

HERE'S THE SECRET SOLUTION: Convert the time you're wasting watching television reruns and use it to develop your own PowerPoint presentation that is 100% in terms of the customer's (or your audience's) needs and desires.

Free Git̊Bit...**Want to see a sample portion of my PowerPoint presentation, "The 31.5 Characteristics of a Winner?"** Send an e-mail to yes@gitomer.com with the word SLIDES in the subject line.

ELEMENT

5

POWER PRESENTATION

"Friends, Romans, and prospective customers... Lend me your credit cards."

The essence of selling yourself to an audience

Here are the 29.5 power elements of presenting:

1. YOU CAN DO IT – IF YOU BELIEVE YOU CAN. Your presentation will only be as good as you believe it will be (and that you have prepared it to be). Many are "afraid" to get up in front of the room. Don't confuse fear with lack of preparation. Fear is a reactive state of mind and can be easily replaced.

2. THEY BUY YOU FIRST. It's about credibility. Yours. They only buy your message if they buy you. You know the old story – don't shoot the messenger. Well, it started from people giving lousy performances. People are not buying your company or your product – they're buying you. If they buy you, your product or your service has a shot. If they don't buy you, your product or your service has no shot. And you get shot.

3. THE INTRODUCTION SETS THE TONE. If it's a low tone, get it up. Write your introduction and get your introducer to practice it. Make it short, impressive, and reassuring.

4. IT'S SHOW BUSINESS – CREATE A MOOD OF UPBEAT EXCITEMENT. Music, slides, video. Put the crowd in the right frame of mind before your talk starts. I play rock music.

5. COMMAND THE ROOM WITH POISE AND AN OPEN AURA.
You are center stage whether it's five seconds or five minutes. Take control. Stand up straight and be proud.

6. DON'T TALK UNTIL YOU HAVE ESTABLISHED RAPPORT AND THE AUDIENCE IS SMILING.
Risk humor so you know their mood and personality.

7. DON'T DEMAND THE AUDIENCE PARTICIPATE.
Don't say "Hello." To which the audience responds with a weak "Hello." And you say "I said HELLO." And they're all pissed because you made them do it and treated them like children. Great, you're less than 20 seconds into the talk, and you've already irritated half the audience.

8. MAKE THEM LAUGH, BUT DON'T TELL A DUMB JOKE.
What's a dumb joke? You'll know one second after you tell it. There will be groans, polite laughter, or (the worst) silence. If the room is laughing, they're buying.

9. SHOULD I USE NOTES?
Do what's comfortable – if it looks cool. Use one-word notes – or work off your handout. Don't fumble – know it cold.

10. YOU GET FIVE EXTRA POINTS FOR LOOKING GOOD.
Dress to suit yourself, but be stylish and neat.

11. ASK ENGAGING QUESTIONS.
Questions about loyalty, finance, technology, use of product, service, quality, or future. Questions about them – that make them think and respond.

12. MAKE THE MESSAGE POWERFUL BY CREATING AND DELIVERING A POWERFUL PRESENTATION. Don't speak without a beginning, a point or two, a laugh, and an ending.

13. MAKE A HIGH-POWERED, CONCISE, COMPELLING PRESENTATION THAT CREATES A DESIRE FOR INVOLVEMENT. One that's rehearsed and presented by someone with professional speaking skills. Audiences have short attention spans. That's why slides are used.

14. ANTICIPATE AUDIENCE QUESTIONS, AND ANSWER THEM IN YOUR PRESENTATION. To build credibility, you must answer (dispel) doubts. Use facts with examples. And tell stories to prove your point.

15. DON'T SAY "UH" OR "UM" EVEN IF YOUR ASS FALLS OFF. Avoid er, um, ah, uh, you know, again (I hate again), and duh. If you have a hitch in your presentation, it will painfully distract the audience. Stupidity is not limited to words. There are dumb gestures, too. Hands in pocket, hair fidget, twitch, jingle something, play with something. To win the crowd, you can't let your flaws detract from your message.

16. THERE ARE ELEMENTS OF PRESENTATION THAT MAKE IT HIT OR MISS (MAKE THE AUDIENCE CHEER OR HISS). Tone, vocal variety, eye contact, enunciation, posture, gestures, and dress combine to allow the clarity of message a chance to shine through. Don't do anything to get in the way of your message.

17. HAVE A PROP OR TWO. I've used a washcloth, a tin cup, a glass, a tube of chapstick, a book, a mirror (handheld), and plastic vomit. Props are fun and help make the point.

18. SLIDES DIVERT ATTENTION – BUT THEY GIVE YOU CREDIBILITY AND AUTHENTICITY. Use them as reinforcement, or to get a laugh or two. The key is not to make your slides bigger than your information. Slides are great if used in an engaging manner. Word of caution: Slides are a risk if you need them and your technology fails. Master your technology capability and always have a backup. Over the years, I have become a huge proponent of slides to complement my talk and create a compelling message. Slides work.

19. TEST THE PARTICIPANTS. You can create incredible desire for your information with a short assessment of the audience's present skill level. Let each person rate their own reality on a scale of 1 to 5 on each question you present. The purpose of self-assessment is to create a black-and-white picture of where they are versus where they want to be as it relates to your message.

20. CREATE A SENSE OF URGENCY. A compelling reason to act now. The ability to create a fear of loss, or a desire to gain, is crucial to your overall success.

21. GET A ROADIE TO PUSH THE BUTTONS, DIM THE LIGHTS, AND PASS OUT THE HANDOUTS. Prepare and arrange everything before the talk begins.

22. ATTENTION SPANS ARE SHORT AND PEOPLE ARE IMPATIENT. Get to the point. Make good points. Make concise points. Ask for a commitment. Thank everyone. Graciously accept your applause. And make an exit.

23. EVEN IF YOU STINK, YOUR STORY CAN SAVE YOU. If you prepare one thing – prepare your story. Tell your own story, not someone else's.

24. CREATE A REAL STORY THAT HAS RELATABLE CONCEPTS.
Something that provokes thought in your audience. Make them laugh, make them think, make them want, make them cry. Then practice using the self-evaluation rehearsal method discussed on page 54 and 55.

25. TELL STORIES WITH PASSION – SHORT AND SWEET.
Make every time you tell your story sound like the first time you told it.

26. SOLICIT SPOKEN TESTIMONIALS OF THOSE WHO HAVE ALREADY ACTED.
The more testimonials, the more you will get your way.

27. HAVE AT LEAST THREE NEW IDEAS THAT DIRECTLY RELATE TO THEM.
If you bring new information, the audience will like you. If you bring new ideas, the audience will love you.

28. TELL THE AUDIENCE THAT THEIR QUESTIONS WILL BE ANSWERED AFTER YOUR PRESENTATION.
Warning: One poorly answered question in front of a group could spoil the entire presentation.

29. END WITH A LAUGH, A TEAR, A POWERFUL STATEMENT, OR...
give someone else the applause with a powerful introduction segue after you're finished.

29.5 CONFIDENCE BREEDS CONFIDENCE.
Yours breeds theirs. The more you own your talk, the greater confidence you will project and the greater audience acceptance you will have.

5

Your audience wants to get to know you, to like you, to have confidence in you, to believe you, to trust you, to understand you, to learn from you, to smile or laugh, and to feel like you value them.

– Jeffrey Gitomer

Some stuff is OK, some is not OK...

- It's **OK** to use notes.
- It's **OK** to use props.
- It's **OK** to use *compelling* slides.
- It's **OK** to stumble.
- It's **OK** to be real.
- It's **OK** to be excited.

- It's **not OK** to be nervous.
- It's **not OK** to be unprepared.
- It's **not OK** to be unrehearsed.
- It's **not OK** to pander to the audience.
- It's **not OK** to make excuses.
- It's **not OK** to ramble on about yourself.
- It's **not OK** to ramble on about nothing and assume anyone is interested.
- It's **not OK** to tell your story unless it relates to your audience.

5

Starting with the best words and phrases

Whenever I watch someone give a speech, or make a presentation, I always listen for their first few words. It tells me what type of presentation they are about to give.

Most presentations are exceptionally ineffective, and even fewer have great beginnings.

The strategy I have always used at the beginning of a talk is one that I refer to as: *start in the middle*. Rather than greet the audience, I begin by telling a story, almost in mid-sentence. The audience is not forced to listen; they're compelled to listen.

If I don't tell a story, I begin with a question. One that I believe most people in the audience can relate to. I'll ask, "How many of you, when you're driving around in your car, listen to the music you grew up with?" And most audience members will raise their hand. I have immediately gained engagement. Not only are people listening, but they're also participating. It's also likely that most people have never heard that question before.

5

I've not only engaged them, I've made them think – and consider new information. After I have asked the question, I make a point. Now they can't wait to hear what I have to say next. After I make a point, I say something funny. I don't tell a joke, I use humor.

Within my first two minutes, I engage the audience, I make them consider new information, I get them to participate, I get them to laugh, and I make a point.

My compelling opening remarks begin to win the audience. To keep the momentum, I continue to use information that will make them think, make engagement statements about them (not me), inject humor as often as possible, and drive home my point with examples and stories.

I also use "opening lines" or "segue lines" to get from one subject to another. By using a pause, I can create new segments. Each time I begin, I'll use a phrase like, "Picture this…" or "How many of you have ever…" and then go on to tell my story and make my point.

POWER NOTE: In delivering my message, one of the most powerful things that I do is separate myself from the audience with pronouns.

Physically, I am next to them. Mentally, I am in tune with them. But verbally, each member of the audience clearly knows that I am in the front of the room – and they are listening and taking notes.

5

As an expert (or THE expert), you must keep your distance from the audience with words – predominantly pronouns. I do this by excluding myself. I don't say "we." I say "you." I don't say "our." I say "your." I don't say "us." I say "you."

By not including myself with the audience, I show confidence rather than vulnerability. I show conviction rather than frailty. And I give hope to them by NOT including myself.

My personal belief is that any speaker, either knowingly or unknowingly, who includes themselves with the audience has both a lack of understanding and a lack of confidence in delivering a message. They seek approval rather than seek to help.

I also believe that it prevents the message from being as persuasive as it could be.

Oftentimes, when a presenter tries to humble himself or herself in front of the audience, it actually comes across as being insincere, or worse, pandering.

In my experience (another phrase I use at the beginning of a talk segment), I have found that audiences are very quick to make judgment on the sincerity and the strength of a message. The presenter or the speaker must disconnect verbally to connect mentally.

5

If you seek to persuade, you must position yourself through stature and language. Both of these elements are achieved when you choose your pronouns carefully.

— Jeffrey Gitomer

Power loss

Why you lose it. How to build it back up.

Speaking in front of a group (of any size) can be anywhere between the most terrifying and most rewarding experience of a lifetime. I'm blessed to have the opportunity to deliver more than 100 speeches a year to some of the largest, most sophisticated audiences in the world. I'm never nervous. Oh, sometimes I get excited. And I'm full of energy every time I speak. But nervous? Never.

It is said that people fear presenting more than dying.

REASON: You're still alive after you give a lousy speech.

I've discovered why presenters (or people who have to give a speech) get "nervous" before and during the event: Nervous and its evil twin "afraid" are symptoms, not problems.

Here are the problems that cause speakers to lose power, to be nervous, and to be afraid:

1. UNPREPARED. If you're not prepared to present, there's an uneasiness and fear of getting "caught" unprepared. Sometimes, it's in the familiarity of the material that you're presenting. Or deeper – it's a lack of *understanding* of the material you're presenting combined with the fear of being asked a question that you don't know the answer to. (Remember high school?)

5

Either way, the remedy is a two-part preparation:

First, you must understand and "own" the material you are presenting. **NOTE:** I did not say memorize. Memorizing is the single biggest cause of fear in presenting – fear of forgetting. If you own it (know it cold), you won't need to memorize it.

Second, prepare a list of questions you anticipate the audience will ask. Then, answer each question on paper. By answering your own questions, you'll give yourself additional knowledge and, at the same time, additional self-confidence.

2. LIMITED SELF-IMAGE. If you think you're not very pretty, weigh too much, are the wrong color, or are too old, you're correct. If you tell yourself you are the greatest and getting better, you are also correct. Your choice. Judge yourself – don't stand in the shadow of the judgment of others.

3. LIMITED SELF-ESTEEM. This differs slightly from low self-image in that you value yourself and your capabilities at a low level. Someone way back told you that you were stupid, or ugly, and you believed them. Big mistake. The cure for limited self-image and low self-esteem is the same. Go out as fast as you can and purchase *The Strangest Secret* by Earl Nightingale. It's a 30-minute lesson about the reality of your self-thinking. While it was recorded in the late '50s, it's still the single, most-powerful personal development message available today. **HINT:** The cure lies in the way you direct your thoughts.

4. AFRAID OF RIDICULE. This is a burned-in image from grade school, junior high school, and high school where some teacher made fun of you in front of the class. Everyone in the class laughed. You felt like dirt. Teachers have no right to ridicule anybody other than themselves.

As a parent, when my daughter was told, "That's a stupid question," I immediately had her removed from that teacher's class. My advice is simple: If you're well prepared, professional looking, and your self-image is high, the fear of ridicule will evaporate over time.

5. LACK OF SELF-CONFIDENCE. This is the most complex of all personality flaws. It's actually a combination of the four previously listed. Confidence is built (or destroyed) over time based on your thinking and life experiences.

As you build small victories, your confidence improves.

When you first tried to ride a two-wheel bike, you were nervous and shaky. The episode no doubt resulted in a fall, a skinned knee, blood, and excessive crying. Within a week, you were riding the bike. And within two weeks, you were riding the bike with no hands – the result of successive, successful experiences.

Free Git Bit...Your successful experiences add to and build your success attitude. To find out more, go to www.gitomer.com, register if you are first-time user, and enter the words SUCCESS ATTITUDE in the GitBit box.

5

POWER UP

The best way to prevent power loss is to have enough power stored so that you can generate it during your talk.

I know that sounds like the electric company. Actually, the two *are* very similar. You have to have a base of mental power and verbal power stored in your mind so that you can generate it as needed during your presentation.

Here are some ideas that will get you on the "fearless" track:

DWELL ON YOUR PAST VICTORIES AND SUCCESSES. Remind yourself of when you did it, not when you didn't.

WRITE DOWN "WHY" YOU HAVE THE FEAR. Many people have fear and are clueless as to the cause. Sometimes, that self-discovery is enough to make it dissipate and disappear.

FEED YOUR HEAD. As I have mentioned, the supreme confidence building answer is in Earl Nightingale's *The Strangest Secret*. I recommend you listen to it once a week for a year, and then once a month for a lifetime. I have... and so far, it's working.

TEST YOUR PROWESS IN A SAFE ATMOSPHERE. Speak for free at your local civic group. All groups that meet weekly need a fifteen-minute speaker. It should be you. Who knows, you may even make a great contact (or two).

PRACTICE ALONE. Walk on a beach and speak to yourself. Sit in your room with the door shut and read aloud. Over time, you will improve. Fifteen minutes a day is all you need.

RECORD YOURSELF. There is no better teacher than a recording of your own voice. You have two options. You can listen to it and think how bad you are, or you can listen to it and note where you can improve and what you can work on. Self-recording is the single-biggest element in self-improvement.

JOIN TOASTMASTERS. Wherever you live, a Toastmasters group is close by. Go to www.toastmasters.org and join a club in your area. Toastmasters provides an easy, fun, inexpensive, non-threatening, and supportive environment for you to improve your presentation skills.

CREATE A PEER GROUP AND GIVE YOUR TALKS TO ONE ANOTHER. Five friends or business associates gathered in a living room once a week giving five-minute presentations to one another is better time spent than watching any TV rerun. It will build confidence, skills, and friendships.

LEAD A COMMITTEE AT A BUSINESS ORGANIZATION. Become a spokesperson. Lead the completion of an idea or project.

HAVE SOME FUN – CALL A RADIO TALK SHOW. It's anonymous and it's a passionate expression – you get to say what you feel. Record it and see how it compares to your other recordings. I'll bet it's better. Reason? Passion requires less front-of-brain thought. It comes from the heart. And that should be a clue – a *big* clue.

5

Tell a story – make a point

Have you ever read *Aesop's Fables*? Aesop was the guy who wrote stories that had a moral. It's important to note that the moral appeared at the end of the story.

Two thousand, five hundred years ago, Aesop was trying to tell you how to be compelling, how to be engaging, how to peak the interest of the audience, how to get the audience to see your point of view, and how to drive your point, or your moral, home.

In short, through the medium of writing, Aesop was able to woo you, wow you, and teach you.

He did it in story form. When you tell a story, the object is for people to agree with you, learn from you, and be persuaded by you – through the parable, metaphor, or similar situation that you're presenting.

CAUTION: Never use the phrase, "Let me tell you a story." Just tell the story. Never preface your story by saying, "This is funny" or "This is hilarious." Let others decide that. Your job is to tell a compelling story and make the audience think and react favorably by making your point at the end.

5

Facts and figures are forgotten. Stories are retold.

– Jeffrey Gitomer

What's so funny about being professional?

There's an old adage that says, "If you can make 'em laugh, you can make 'em buy." The reason it's old and the reason its been around so long is that its true.

Humor and laughter are two key ingredients in gaining engagement and building a relationship.

The challenge with humor is people don't know how or when to use it. They're afraid to use it because they think it will make them look unprofessional.

Let me dispel that misguided thought of fear with the following 4.5 reasons to inject more humor into your presentation and your life:

1. Humor is the final frontier. It's easy to learn about your audience. It's easy to learn how to present. But it's hard to learn the science of humor. And it's harder to learn how to place and time that humor into your presentation. Humor creates a more open atmosphere – that atmosphere will breed friendship, respect, and compatibility.

5

The reason I refer to it as the final frontier is because it's the last element that you put into your speaking process. You put it in only after you're the master of your material.

2. Humor is the highest form of language mastery. If you've heard someone say, "Boy, that guy's funny. He's a natural at it," it's likely the guy is an extremely intelligent human.

If you learn a foreign language, the last thing you do is learn the humor, and the hardest thing to do is make a joke. Humor is the most difficult of nuances to master. But when you do, you have the basis for solid, intellectual rapport and engagement.

3. What's so funny about being professional? If your entire talk is professional, you are likely to lose to someone who's talk is 50% professional and 50% friendly combined with funny. Friendly and funny are a thousand times more engaging than professional.

If you doubt that, take a look at any late-night TV host. Are they professional or funny? How much are they making? How much are you making? I don't mean to compare your presentation to a David Letterman monologue, but I am challenging you to compare the way you think you have to present to the way your audience would like to be presented to.

I have incorporated professional talk with funny talk for the last 30 years. Not only has it made me a ton of sales, it has also made me a ton of friends. It will do the same for you.

5

4. The difference between a joke and a story. Most people reduce themselves to joke tellers, or should I say, "joke re-tellers," or should I say, "bad joke re-tellers." Joke telling is dangerous and usually not very funny for three reasons. First, most jokes are demeaning to one person or another. Second, jokes sound contrived, almost like you're trying too hard. And third (worst), if the audience has heard the joke before, it makes you look like a complete idiot, especially after the joke when you're the only one laughing.

Stories, on the other hand, are genuine. They tell about experience, they can use self-effacing humor, and they're engaging. When you tell a great story, it makes the listener think of a story to engage you with. (In storytelling, that's called a "topper.") If you can make each person in the audience think of their own story as a result of listening to yours, that's a rapport builder.

4.5 Laughter is universal. The use of humor is almost never taught. The reason is that most training and most trainers aren't that funny. I'm not saying that if you're not funny, you're not valid. But I am saying that if I'm in a selling situation against you, and I'm funny and you're professional, or I'm funny and you're not funny, I will win the sale more often. If you don't consider yourself a funny person, study humor or read about how to become more humorous.

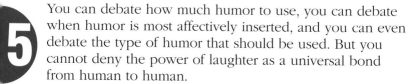

You can debate how much humor to use, you can debate when humor is most affectively inserted, and you can even debate the type of humor that should be used. But you cannot deny the power of laughter as a universal bond from human to human.

The late George Burns once said, "With the death of vaudeville, new comedians have no place to stink." What he meant was to be great at humor, you have to try it out and be willing to fail at it.

Just because you fail to get a laugh a few times doesn't mean you should quit at it. Humor takes time, humor takes intelligence, humor takes trial and error, humor takes practice, and humor helps you get your way.

"Always start your presentation with a joke.
But be careful not to offend anyone! Don't mention religion,
politics, race, money, disease, technology, men, women,
children, plants, animals, food…"

The gift of gab

Do you have "the gift of gab?"

I've had it all my life and thought I was pretty good at it *until* I learned the science of selling and discovered "controlled gab." I became more proficient at gab when I created an engaging personal commercial. I mastered gab when I began speaking in public.

Roy Rogers (a famous cowboy from the '50s) had a sidekick named George "Gabby" Hayes. Personifying his nickname, Gabby was constantly talking. Very little of his gab was appreciated, or listened to, because he was always "gabbing." It was comical, but sad. And when he had something really important to say, he had to scream or repeat himself several times before anyone would listen or take him seriously.

Making a presentation? In reality, you're trying to persuade. You may call it a presentation, but that's the worst name for it because it sets the wrong thought process in your mind.

You're not presenting, you're persuading.

You're uncovering needs. You're trying to build value.

5

You're trying to gain audience trust by being likeable, being believable, and transferring confidence.

That doesn't sound like a presentation to me. It sounds more like a concerted effort that takes a ton of preparation combined with an extraordinary level of presentation skills.

I recently read a book on making presentations. I'm not going to mention the name of it, or the author. But suffice it to say, the book was expensive and the content was pathetic. It went through the presentation process from the author's perspective – certainly not what's necessary in the real world.

Some of the tips offered in the book were, "it's good to be nervous," "don't try to be perfect," "know your subject," and "practice, practice, practice." *Where's the beef?*

Those lessons are in a book – and they're silly. They have nothing to do with making a successful presentation, a dynamic presentation, or a winning presentation.

If you go into a presentation and you're nervous, in my book, that's not okay. You have to go into a presentation reeking of confidence. The reason people are nervous is because they are unprepared. And being unprepared is one of the best ways that I know to lose an audience.

When I see a rule like "don't try to be perfect," I always think to myself...*exactly where would you like me to screw up? In the beginning? When I'm delivering the meat?*

When you're giving a presentation, "knowing your subject" is a given. The rule should be "know your audience or you will die a thousand presentation deaths."

What you need to know is how your audience can benefit and profit from what you are presenting.

When an expert tells me to "practice, practice, practice," the first question I want to know is, "practice what?"

What it should say is "build your presentation skills daily by giving presentations and recording them."

When you've done the recording, play it back immediately.

If you've ever wanted a dose of reality, I promise you that playing back your presentation will be the funniest, most pathetic thing you have ever heard. It is the grimmest dose of reality for most people.

When you record yourself, it's exact evidence of what you said, how you said it, how impactful it was, how transferable it was, how persuasive it was, how convincing it was, and, ultimately, how successful it was.

5

The average person (not you, of course) is presentation weak. This is predominantly caused by lack of study, lack of preparation, and lack of recording.

Recording your presentation will reveal every blemish, every error, and every weakness. It will give you a report card on your effectiveness.

NOTE: Your presentation skills are a big part of the getting your way process. It's where your personal preparation meets the opportunity of being in front of someone who can say "Yes" to you.

Wouldn't you think, with all this at stake, that presentation skills would be one of the highest priorities in a person's life?

5

Well, luckily for you, the average person doesn't feel that way. The average person is at home right after work hunting around for the TV remote instead of hunting up new facts for the presentation tomorrow. He's hunting for a can of beer instead of hunting for a Toastmasters meeting.

If you would like to rise above 95% of all people in the marketplace, then begin now by studying presentation skills. Book a few speeches at your local Rotary or Kiwanis Club. Try to speak at a trade show instead of just exhibiting there.

And whatever you do, **record whatever you say**.

Recording is the *best* and *only* way to examine your present skill level and to make your game plan for improvement.

HERE'S THE BEST PART: If you want a report card, all you have to do is look at how often you're able to get your way. As your presentation skills increase, your frequency of getting your way will increase proportionately. It may even increase disproportionately.

Wouldn't that be a nice present?

Free GitBit...Want more tips about presentation skills? I've got a few more. Go to www.gitomer.com, register if you are a first-time user, and enter the word PRESENT in the GitBit box.

ELEMENT

6

PERSUASION PERFORMANCE

"I have to give a presentation today and I'm nervous."

"No, you don't! You have to give a PERFORMANCE today and you're nervous because you're unprepared."

Speech, speech!

I give about 120 speeches per year and have done so for the last 15 years. That's about 1,800 speeches.

Here are what I've discovered to be the 8.5 elements of what you have to do to deliver a "standing ovation" and "Yes-generating" quality speech:

1. INFORM THE AUDIENCE. This assumes you will be presenting "new" information. Information the listener can use to produce more, or profit more. Information that has no self-serving commercial content but speaks to your expertise in your area of commerce.

2. ENTERTAIN THE AUDIENCE. You have a responsibility to inform *and* entertain. No one wants to listen to a boring speech. The secret to entertaining the audience is *make them laugh*.

3. GET THEM TO LAUGH AND THEY WILL LISTEN. Ever been to a comedy club? The comedian tells a joke and you laugh until the drink is coming out your nose. The comedian begins to talk again, and you immediately stifle your laugh until it hurts you so you can hear the next joke. At the end of laughter is the height of listening.

4. THERE MUST BE AT LEAST ONE AHA! Something in your talk that makes the audience realize new and important information for the first time. They must listen to your words, thoughts, and ideas – and say or think, "AHA!"

5. GIVE THE AUDIENCE HOPE. Everyone wants a better life, a better job, more money, and the HOPE that they can achieve their desires. The key word here is *encouragement*.

6. EXTRACT EMOTION FROM THE AUDIENCE BY SHARING YOURS. Your message, however long or short, must be compelling. Your belief in your words must be evident to all.

7. TRANSFER MESSAGES AND IDEAS TO THE AUDIENCE. People must think: "I get it. I think I can do it. I'm willing to try it." At that point, your message has transferred to the listener.

8. DON'T MOTIVATE THE AUDIENCE, INSPIRE THEM. Motivation lasts a moment. Inspiration lasts for years.

8.5 OWN YOUR TALK. Know it like you know your name and all your nervousness will be gone. When you own the talk, you don't have to be "in the talk." You can be "in the room" with the audience.

If you give a great talk, people will thank you, act on it, tell others about it, and remember it for years.

It's not just a presentation. It's a performance!

6

Think about the last time you went to a concert, a play, or some other performing arts event. You sat there glued to your seat, leaning forward, totally engaged because it was a *performance*, not a presentation.

Think about your presentation. Are you performing, or just presenting? Theatrical people put their heart, their energy, their skill, and their passion into their performance. They seek to master their art. And, they're constantly looking to improve.

Some performances are so good and so compelling that you will remember them, and talk about them, forever.

I challenge you, as I challenge every person I come in contact with, to put your heart into your presentation and turn it into a performance.

As with all endeavors of persuasion, there's a secret that will get you from where you are – to the next level of excellence. The secret is *practice with passion*.

But it's not that simple. If you don't love what you do, practicing will be a chore. If you love it, practicing won't just be fun – it will be something you look forward to.

How to deliver the greatest ~~presentation~~ in the world
performance

6

The old adage is, "It's not what you say – it's how you say it." Wrong. It's both. To convert a great presentation into a performance, it takes the perfect marriage of what you say and how you say it – or the audience will divorce you.

I'm going to concentrate on how you say it (the squeak). If you deliver the greatest presentation in the world with no enthusiasm, sincerity, or belief – you'll lose.

In the beginning of a performance, there are four elements that determine whether you'll get your way:

1. Rapport. Putting yourself on the same side of the fence with the audience. Can they relate to you?

2. Need. Determining what the audience deems as the factors that will influence their motivation to listen with the intent to act. Do your words fulfill their needs?

3. Importance. The transferability and urgency of your message. Are they willing to try it?

4. Confidence. Your ability to gain comfort and build assurance that there is limited risk and maximum reward for seeing the message your way. Can they relate?

6

While all the information from these elements can be acquired by asking the right questions, the difference between good and great performers is the way they present (deliver) their message.

Much is said about techniques to coerce or persuade. Not much is said (or written) about performance skills, also known as your fundamental communication competence, combined with public speaking adeptness, to blend a symphonic (persuasion) pitch.

Your speaking skills must be used throughout the entire performance, but they're critical at the start because they create an impression and set a tone for the rest of the performance.

I've compiled a list of essential skills and definitions for implementation.

Here are the strategic elements of "how you say it":

- **Speak clearly.** Sounds simple, but if the audience doesn't understand you (accent, dialect, speak too fast, jump around), your communication won't be understood, and you won't get your way.

- **Lean forward.** Lean into the performance to give the listener the sense of importance and urgency.

- **Don't fidget.** Knuckle-cracking, pocket-jingling, or other nervous habits detract from the performance.

6

- **Don't fumble.** Fumbling around means you're not prepared. It makes the audience feel on edge and act impatient. It also makes them unsure of you.

- **Don't "um," "ah," or "er."** Vocalized pauses, hesitations, and repeated words are so irritating. They make the audience focus on flaws rather than the message. The biggest cure for this is practice.

- **Be animated.** Wide eyed, as though you just had the most fantastic thing happen to you.

- **Use lots of hand gestures.** Not wild hand-waving. Pointed, compelling gestures.

- **Use a wide range of vocal variety.** Loud and soft voices. Not singing, but close. Go from high to low tones. Punch the critical words. Compel the audience to listen. Say it with style.

- **Whisper some important stuff like it's a secret.** Get the prospect to lean into your words. Make him or her feel special to get your message.

- **Stand up when you perform.** It adds impact to your gestures and to the story.

- **Stand up (sit up) straight.** Posture determines the direction of your words. If you're stoop-shouldered, your words are spoken to the floor instead of to the audience.

- **Look them in the eye.** Your eye contact is a tell-tale sign of credibility to the audience. Use direct eye contact. Looking the other person in the eye is a confidence builder.

- **Take performance risks.** Don't perform in a shell. Say new things. Invent new methods of performance on the spot. It may mean that you get a bit uncomfortable. So what? That's how you grow.

- **Stay within the range of your audience's personality.** If the audience is stuffy and conservative, don't get too wild.

- **Say your words with conviction.** Self-belief will account for a large portion of getting your way.

- **Select the right words.** Sound intelligent. You don't have to quote Shakespeare, but you do need to be a wordsmith. Use industry buzzwords. Build ten new words into your vocabulary every week.

- **Emphasize important words.** When you come to a critical word or phrase – punch it and pause to let it sink in.

- **Use your entire body.** Gesture with your hands and arms. Get up and walk around the room. Shift your weight for emphasis of a point.

- **Nod yes.** This small subliminal body language technique is among the most powerful. It sets a mood of "yes" throughout the performance.

- **Smile.** This isn't brain surgery; it's helping other people. It's fun. Your facial expression of smile makes the prospect feel good inside.

- **Relax.** High anxiety makes the audience nervous. As previously stated (three times), the main reason people are nervous is they are unprepared (or they need money). Calm down. Never let them see (or feel) you sweat.

Be prepared to screw up several performances as you begin your quest for eloquence.

Look at it as a journey, not as a speech, and realize that you'll only get from acceptable to good to great to greatest over an extended period of time.

But you can't get there unless you start.

You are the vehicle.
You are the messenger.

I'm providing you the fuel and the message.
The rest is up to you.

Skill, or vital necessity?

"Business owners, executives, managers, and salespeople fail to realize how much of their success is dependent on the way they speak. Poor speaking habits can destroy credibility," says Ty Boyd, founder of the Excellence in Speaking Institute (Charlotte, North Carolina).

"Most people don't realize how weak their presentation skills really are – and how easy it is to reverse the process if they just focus on themselves and their message."

Great advice from a master.

How many of you will take the challenge to raise your skills and improve? Need a push? The best methods of putting fire in your throat without being perceived as a dragon are below.

Here are 9.5 success tactics of how to get ready, get great at performing, and get your way:

1. Get a grip. Shake hands so firmly that the other person notices. A solid handshake sets a confident aura around you from the first moment of contact.

2. Set the mood. It's your responsibility as a great communicator to create an atmosphere where information can flow comfortably and naturally.

3. Pace your delivery. Get a feel for time and timing. Regulate and balance your timing between the needs and desires of your audience. One of the biggest mistakes people make is going too quickly or talking too fast. Even though you're giving your presentation for the 1,000th time, the audience is hearing it for the first time.

4. Tag team for evaluation purposes. Have a co-worker or boss go with you once a week, and make them listen. Create a review form (see page 54 and 55) and have it filled out immediately after your performance. Talk about what you could do to improve. Write down your strengths and your weaknesses.

5. Record your telephone conversations. Use them as a self-monitor of your ability to present a clear and confident message. Play them back, if you dare. If you can't stand your voice, change your pitch.

6. Read and record a chapter from any of my books onto a CD. Play it in your car. You'll learn about sales *and* about how you present. Would you be compelled to listen to you? If not, record another one with style and emotion.

7. Videotape your opening five minutes. Invite a friend or co-worker to review the tape with you. Watch the video and rate your performance. Have a sickness bag (or two) from an airline nearby because when you see yourself, you'll puke – or deny it's you. Repeat the process once a week for two months.

8. Be your own video critic once a week. Watch your own tape at home. Work to eliminate the two worst habits, and at the same time, work to enhance your two best strengths.

9. Be prepared. Know your message cold. Rehearse your words before you perform them. Get comfortable with your process and your story.

9.5. Be yourself. Don't put on an act. Your personality will shine if you believe in what you are saying. Being genuine will win the confidence of the audience.

"Being yourself means being willing to lose everything for the sake of your beliefs and ideals."

Elements of presentation that, when mastered, lead to a performance

VOCAL VARIETY. Your tone of expression creates the desire to listen, or not. When you perform your words, you're almost singing them in a variety of tones. This allows you to both yell and whisper, and to emphasize those words that are most important, while still presenting a clear and complete message. Your history professor may have been brilliant, but if he spoke in monotone, no one listened. I didn't.

GESTURES. The wider – the better. Use your arms, not just your hands. And practice by video recording every chance you get. Each time you watch, look to see if your gestures are natural or contrived. Let your arms flow with your words and let your hands go along for the ride. Personally, I don't "think" about my gestures, I just let them come naturally. And I believe that they appear to be more genuine and more sincere when they just flow. Gestures emphasize words and create interaction. Gestures make your talk, and your words, come alive.

BODY LANGUAGE. Lean forward. My style has often been described as "in your face." I like that description because it means that I have made direct contact with the audience. And it means that I am most likely to be listened to and understood. Some people might refer to it as blunt, but I perform with a combination of words and body.

6

The words are bold, and my body positioning matches the words. Your body language exposes and expresses your confidence and your self-belief.

EYE CONTACT. You cannot look at the audience. You must look at a person. Not one person all the time. Rather, make eye contact with people, one at a time. When you combine body language with eye contact, you get the true meaning of the words "in your face." You're leaning forward and looking someone right in the eye. Not only does this create a compelling message, but it also shows that you believe in what you're saying and have the confidence to look directly at someone. Eye contact gives the audience a warmer feeling about you – even if your audience is only one person. Eye contact also connotes trust. You've heard the expression, "He couldn't even look me in the eye." If you're looking for a way to begin turning presentation into performance, the eyes have it.

CLARITY OF WORDS. Growing up in Philadelphia, I was exposed to "the Philly" accent. "Wanna" instead of "Want to." "Gonna" instead of "Going to." To make matters worse, half of my family was from Philly, the other half was from Brooklyn. Yada, Yada. My mother stood in the middle as the champion of diction, ever correcting the way I spoke. One of the biggest compliments I get is when people tell me, "You have no accent." I just smile and thank my mom. The clarity of your words determine their impact and their transferability. If you have ever sat in the front row of a Broadway show, you have seen the performers spitting or spraying as they sing or talk. That's clarity – in *performance* format.

Now, I'm not saying, "Spit on the people you talk to." I am saying, "Be aware of how you pronounce words." (Especially if you have an accent or tend to use the idiomatic expressions that you grew up with.)

SOUL. Soul has 500 definitions. From a getting your way perspective, I'm going to define it as *your ability to be smooth and in harmony with yourself.* It's the way you combine your words with your gestures – your internal swagger. It's the way you perform in a pleasing and acceptable manner. While I believe everyone has inherent characteristics, I also believe that soul can be learned slowly over time. It's easier to develop soul if you have a deep love for what you do. Love and passion lead to soul. And soul will drive you from presentation to performance.

"I was floating in a tunnel toward a very bright light and then a voice told me I had to wake up and finish listening to the presentation."

Karaoke and getting a standing ovation

People are always asking me where I learned my performance skills. I learned to perform better singing karaoke in bars, and I chose to do it without alcohol.

Oh sure, before I began singing karaoke I had given lots of speeches, but I never really understood what I was doing until I began to sing in bars.

When you sing in a karaoke bar, you already know the song, and the words are right in front of you. Even if you can't sing one note, the words are there as a guide, or a crutch. It's hard to fail – unless you can't read.

HERE'S THE SECRET: When you know the song, and you have the words on a screen, you can concentrate on your performance. How you gesture, your body movements, your eye contact, even how you hold the microphone. And you belt it out, because you're in a bar having a good time. Your inhibitions are down.

From 1989 until 1993 I sang karaoke at a variety of clubs in Charlotte – two or three nights a week. Never drank a beer. Always took my laptop. I just went to sing and write in between songs.

One night, one of the singers had a great voice but zero performance skills. I motioned him over after his song and asked if he was interested in getting a standing ovation the next time he sang. He said, "Yes!"

I said, *"Do these four things:"*

1. **Take the microphone (cordless) with you out into the audience and sing out there instead of at the podium.** Join the crowd.

2. **Don't look at the words on the screen; look at the people in the crowd.** You already know the words. Sing to the people, not to the television screen.

3. **Put a little passion into your song.** Use your arms and your body when you sing.

4. **Finish big. Lean back. Hold the last note.** Put your soul into it.

People were screaming at the end of this kid's next performance. Standing and screaming. And the singer's life was changed forever.

I realized that there was more to karaoke than singing a song. I knew that if I kept taking notes while people were singing, I could create a course on "converting presentation skills to performance skills using karaoke."

Over the next two years, here's what I discovered:

The realities...

- Singing sets a positive and relaxed mood in your own mind.

- Because you know (and can see) the words, you can concentrate on the process of performing.

- Too often people concentrate on what they say and forget to communicate. Singing increases communication effectiveness.

- Fast and slow songs have different dynamics. Rock and country songs have different dynamics. If you're a bad singer, don't sing a slow song.

- The audience wants to be entertained. And they are receptive, even if you can't sing. Sometimes the worst singers get the biggest ovation.

- The audience knows the song you're singing. They're singing along. They're in your groove.

- In presenting and performing, there's a big difference between good and dynamic. Singing brings this out immediately.

The concept...

- I could use singing as a metaphor (transfer medium) to teach speaking. Coaching speech dynamics is a snap when related to a song, and it's a performance.

The opportunities...

- Becoming a verbal performing artist.
- Realizing you're a performer not a speaker.
- Being challenged to stand up to the audience.
- Being challenged to make eye contact with people in the audience.
- Singing accentuates performance – not speaking.
- You already know the words. You'll remember them for 50 years. Now perform them.
- How much are you willing to *go for it*?
- Can you get them to dance? (Fast is easy – slow is harder.)
- Can you get the audience to clap (participate)?

If you have a cordless microphone, singing can get you out from behind the small karaoke screen (the podium) and give you a chance to interact with the crowd.

The benefits of singing instead of talking...

6

- It makes you stretch and gets you out of your comfort zone.

- Your back up (music) is there. You sound great, even if you can't sing.

- It allows you to pick out someone and sing to them (one-to-one adds dynamics). When you sing the song to the group, they may not pay attention. When you sing to one person, the entire audience is paying attention and gets the transference.

- It tells you the key to sing in, sets your vocal tone, and makes you concentrate on your verbal (vocal) tone.

- It sets your tempo, your vocal speed, and helps your consistency.

- Your rhythm makes your gestures congruent with words.

- Your gestures are wider and more active – they flow; not jerk. If you do it singing; why wouldn't (don't) you do it speaking?

- It loosens you up.

- You put your entire body into the message.

- It puts melody to your (verbal-vocal) message.

- It makes you use your voice to its maximum capability – its full range of vocal variety.

6

- You see the words in front of you (confidence builder).
- You're familiar with and remember the words.
- It shows you the value of dual eye-contact impact training (the audience versus the individual).
- It's back-up, harmony, and support all at the same time.

It's all about you…

- You're performing in a new way.
- You're the star.
- You're in show (off) business, which takes you to the edge.
- It doesn't matter if you can sing.
- Your coach is always there.
- You can spot your mistakes in a second.
- You can feel yourself get better.
- It's fun.
- It's fun to practice.
- The more fun you have – the better you get.
- Speaking by comparison is easy.
- You're in tune with your song, your rhythm, your message, your audience, and yourself.

6

Transfer the power of understanding and involvement to the audience...

- The message is melodic not verbal.

- Music gets the audience in a great mood.

- Music gets the audience to listen.

- The song has a message – it often has lyrics that you identify with.

- The audience can identify with your message (may evoke their memories).

- If the audience likes your song, they like you (and vice versa).

- If you are introduced to an audience, the introducer sets the tone. If there's music, the music sets the tone.

Want powerful speaking skills?

Singing will determine
if they're *to be*,
or *not to be*.

Film yourself. It's the only way

6

In 1993, I gave a speech to the exhibitors at a trade show – a three-hour presentation on how to make more contacts and make more sales. Having been to hundreds of trade shows, I felt I had pretty good expertise and a pretty good handle on what to say and how to say it.

The woman putting on the event called me and asked, "Would you mind if we videotape your presentation?" I was flattered. I had never been videotaped before, and I told her that if I received a master copy, I would be happy to let her do it. I thought to myself, *I could actually make a product out of this and sell it for big money!*

When the speech was over, everyone applauded. I thought I did a *great* job. I was handed a VHS recording of my talk. That night, I popped some popcorn, called the cat, inserted the VHS, clicked on the machine, and sat back in my easy chair to watch the king.

After fifteen minutes of watching my three-hour presentation, I was gripping the arm of my chair so hard that I couldn't remove my fingers. In short, I sucked. No, I mean, I *really* sucked. I was arrogant, condescending, unsmiling, my clothes looked bad, and I was losing my hair.

6

Any way I looked at it, the sight was not a pretty one. I watched with pain for the next 2 hours and 45 minutes. It was awful. The cat even ran away. But I decided to watch again. This time I took notes.

I made a list of everything I did wrong, entered it into my computer, printed it out, and carried it with me for the next three years. Every time I gave a talk, I would read the list before my talk and then keep it right in front of me on my table or podium. Smile was so important that I put it at the top and bottom of the list.

The moral of the story is *if you don't film yourself, you'll never know how good or bad you are.*

Recording myself gave me reality and a reality check, and it provided a platform for me to learn and improve. Had my talk not been recorded that day, I would have never known the power of recording, and I would have walked away thinking I did a great job – kind of like you do.

I don't know you. I thank you for buying my book – but it's likely I don't know you personally. I am willing to bet you that you don't have a videotape of you giving a performance. Funny, if I asked you how good you are, you would probably say, "I'm pretty good." I would respond and say, "Without a videotape, you have no idea."

Recording your performance is the best and only way to determine your reality and provide yourself the opportunity to get better. I did, and I did.

ELEMENT

7

SALES
PERSUASION
PERFORMANCES

"If you're not in sales, read this section anyway. You'll love it!"

"Woof!"

Major performance clues that lead to a sale

Got a BIG appointment? Want (or need) the sale?

Sure you do. Everyone wants to make the sale, especially when it's a BIG one.

HERE'S THE GOOD NEWS: This it *not* about "how to make a sale." The next three pages contain elements of a sale that engage the prospect. It's much more powerful than your typical "probe, present, overcome objections, close, follow up."

These elements go way beyond your "system" of selling. They go way beyond traditional selling. These elements are for professionals who want to build relationships – not just make a sale. These elements will make the prospect respect you. These elements will lead to partnering. These elements will make the prospect want to buy from you.

Here are 11.5 major elements that you must incorporate into your sales performance:

1. Develop a belief system in your company, your product or service, and yourself that's so strong that you assume every sale before you walk in the door. This mental mindset is the single most powerful element you can possess. If belief is weak, the passion will be weak, and the prospect won't catch your fire.

2. Do your homework the night before. Prepare ideas to help the customer produce more and profit more. Being ready with ideas that can help the prospect will breed your own self-confidence. You'll feel ready to win and be geared up to get your way.

3. Prerelax. Set your own internal tone. Listen to your favorite music on the way over. Be bouncy and in high spirits.

4. Set your mind on helping them achieve their objectives, NOT selling your stuff. That will set a game plan and the agenda for the meeting at the same time.

5. Tell the prospective customer you have come with a few ideas that will help them. This immediately separates you from the others. The prospect will be engaged and listening from the beginning.

6. Make friends with the people you are presenting to before you begin your formalized talk. Become likeable. If they don't like you, you have greatly reduced the probability of them buying from you. Make small talk that allows you to find something in common. It helps everyone relax, and if you're lucky enough, or smart enough, to find a "link" (something of mutual passion), you have set the tone for a positive outcome and the beginning of a relationship – not a sales presentation.

If they aren't smiling, if they aren't friendly at the beginning of the meeting, DIG IN. You're not likely to make the sale without a price fight. Strictly business means strictly price.

7. Ask ONE killer question at the beginning. One that makes the prospect stop and think, consider new information, and respond in terms of you. Get them to respond with their past experience or their opinion. Get them thinking. Get them involved. And earn their respect with questions.

8. Create points of value and areas of differentiation as you're speaking. It's like a prize fight. You have to win each round so that you can win the contest. You don't have to knock them out – you just have to get the decision.

9. Don't "need" the sale. If it's the end of the month, if it's a big customer, and it's a "must" sale, it's likely that you will telegraph this fact to your prospect if it's on your mind. You'll be trying too hard, pressing and pressuring for a "now" answer. You'll try to manipulate the sale so that it can be completed within your quota period. There are a number of worse mistakes in sales, but I am hard pressed to think of one at this moment. By the way, the reason you're pressing is that your pipeline of prospects and prospective customers is empty.

10. Remember all the sales you have already made. Keep your mind set on the winner that you are. But keep your focus on helping the customer win for themselves. The more the prospect feels "they win," the more likely they will buy. When in doubt, ask more questions. When in doubt, think long term.

11. Don't be afraid to ask for the sale. That's why you came, remember?

11.5 While you are qualifying them, they are qualifying you.

This is a secret that most salespeople never realize and are never taught. From the way you enter the room, from the way you look, from the way you treated the administrative person at the front desk, from the first words you speak, the prospect is judging you and deciding who you are as a person. And they're deciding if they want to do business with you. Not your company, not your product, not your service, they are deciding on YOU!

"I always come naked to sales presentations so that you can see that I have no hot buttons you can push!"

What is the BEST way to make a sales presentation?

Getting your way is selling yourself, your ideas, and your product or service to others.

"But Jeffrey," you whine, "I'm not in sales."

Every element of getting your way in some way contains an element of selling. In a job interview, you're selling yourself. When you apply for a bank loan, you're selling your ability to repay the loan and you're also selling your story. As a parent, you're selling your ideas and your authority to your children. As a spouse, you're selling the long-term value of your relationship and your ability to co-relate.

If you're in business and your banker says no to a loan, you must then turn to your vendor to give you credit so that you can continue. You must sell your worth and persuade your worth to the vendor, or you will have a crisis.

In the hiring process, sometimes the employee is selling himself to the company, and sometimes the company is selling itself to the employee. Think about your co-workers or your employees – persuasion takes place in all types of performance, task completion, and self-improvement, all of which require some form of salesmanship.

Every form of business, every form of life, and every form of getting your way contains salesmanship.

In your family life, look to your children as the best salespeople on the planet.

Why do you think they let girl scouts sell cookies instead of mothers? Because kids can outsell mothers 100 to 1. They have more enthusiasm, they have more passion, and they haven't been discouraged by life (yet).

After a seminar the other day, someone asked me why I'm so relaxed when I present. I said, "I'm not worried about what I have to say next. I'm well-prepared for the presentation. I'm experienced at giving presentations to large groups. I don't have stage fright. And I love what I do." There, that answers that.

One minute later, someone else remarked how intense and well-focused I was. How is this possible? One guy says "relaxed," next guy says "intense." I had to stop and think about it.

As I thought back through several thousand sales and platform performances over the past few years, the answer became more obvious. I'm always ready, I'm always relaxed, I always know why I'm there, and I always know what I want.

I answered the "intense" comment with, "I want to make sure my message gets through and that I'm delivering it with as much passion as I am able." "It's not 100 percent," I said. "It's about fifty-fifty. Fifty intense and fifty relaxed." (I guessed.) Sometimes it's sixty-forty, but the point is that there's lot of both.

My response was a revelation about the selling process that will help you understand *how* to make a better presentation and create a buying atmosphere at the same time.

Relax is the mode.

Intense is the focus on your ability to help others and your objective for being there: the sale, the prize, getting your way.

Intense-relaxation seems to be impossible to do at once, but if you're well-prepared, the relax mode is mentally allowing you to focus on the objective rather than the information. And, you can concentrate on the objective with a contagious confidence.

Intense preparation is the key. It takes away nervous and breeds confidence at the same time. You are ready to win. And, it allows you to "drive" for the sale, not "hope" for it.

Nervous people are unprepared people. Or they're people who have failed to transfer their fear of failure into excitement for success. Well-prepared people can convert nervous energy into focused energy – intensity.

RELAX SECRET ONE: When I perform for a group, I never walk out cold. Before the event starts, I mingle and shake as many hands with a smile as I can. If there are 500 people in the room, I've shaken 100 hands with a look-in-the-eye-smile and a brief comment to elicit a returned look-and-smile. *What can you do to relax before you start?*

RELAX SECRET TWO: A HUGE rule of presenting to a group or one-on-one is *make friends first or don't start*. Friends have a better chance for communication without stress or manipulation. *What can you do to make friends first?*

RELAX SECRET TWO POINT FIVE: Relaxation lets the message get through – it's more like a conversation than a sales pitch. *You are relaxed* and *the atmosphere is relaxed.*

INTENSE SECRET ONE: In your sales presentation, you have to bring your own mental arsenal with you. Passion, self-belief, belief in company and product, previous self-success *and* sales success, and a deep knowledge that no question can throw you off the focus track of your self-belief. *How sharp are your mental sales tools?*

INTENSE SECRET TWO: Concentration on getting the message across with maximum impact and believability makes the message contagious – if you can do it in a relaxed atmosphere, that's balance, baby. *How contagious is your message?*

INTENSE SECRET TWO POINT FIVE: If you have prepared your inner focus to help them decide to buy, and it's in harmony with your self-belief and your self-confidence, then you can begin to practice *intense relaxation*.

It never ceases to amaze me how simple sales really is. It doesn't get complicated until someone tells you there's a "system" that will work. Bull. And sales really gets complex when you spend a week learning the system. More bull. But it doesn't get stupid until you try to put the system into your sales presentation, and you lose focus – concentrating on the system, rather than how to help. Most bull. Sales bull.

7

MY WAY IS REAL SIMPLE: Get ready, make friends, know your stuff, know your objective, and relax. Then, repeat the process.

"Above all, be sincere—even if you have to fake it!"

Free Git✗Bit...**Want a list of contributing factors to stress *and* the relaxation counter balances?** Go to www.gitomer.com, register if you are a first-time user, and enter the word STRESS in the GitBit box.

Your friendliness combined with the passion and conviction of your self-belief allows your presentation to be positively received.

— Jeffrey Gitomer

Can't get your way?
Can't close the sale?
Whose fault is that?

7

Are you blaming the prospect when you can't close a sale? Are you telling your boss it's the prospects fault that you can't set an appointment? Or that they won't order now? Or that your price is too high?

After 25 years of selling, training, and consulting, one truth remains – I have yet to hear a salesperson say, "The prospect wouldn't buy and it was *my fault*" or "The prospect wouldn't appoint me and it was *my fault*."

"But Jeffrey, you don't understand. My situation is different." Bull blank. The only thing different about your situation is that you would rather blame someone other than yourself.

IF YOUR PROSPECT IS CONSTANTLY TELLING YOU...

> "Why don't you call back in two weeks?"
>
> "We haven't had a chance to discuss it. Call back in three days."
>
> "Yeah, we're still interested, but it's been real crazy here and...."
>
> "I have to get together with my partner."
>
> "I'm not ready to buy yet."

IT AIN'T THEIR FAULT, VERNE. IT'S YERS.

The key is to accept responsibility for "no sale yet," and ask questions to get the prospect to tell you more about why he is not deciding. He has not said no, so obviously you have just not answered his questions.

People are worrying about, thinking about, or acting on their stuff. You're worrying about, thinking about, or acting on your stuff. Prospects could care less about your stuff unless they perceive the need or a benefit to themselves. It's selfish, but true.

When a prospect says, "I'll know by Thursday at one o'clock," it becomes a benchmark time and date for the salesperson – a deadline. When you come to understand that the date and time commitment means virtually nothing to the prospect, you're on your way to accepting responsibility as a salesperson.

When you follow up the next time, take a proactive stance to hold them to what they said. If they're going to decide by Tuesday, ask, "Could I drop by Wednesday at ten o'clock to get the good news in person?"

At some point, after you have been through the close several times with the prospect, you have to realize that you have very little to lose. You may have to be real direct and ask them if they are going to buy or not. You can't keep wining and dining them for the next year. It's not worth the time or effort.

Well, what if they are just the kind of person who hates to say no? Be up front with them but be understanding as well. You still need to ask the questions to find out why they are postponing the decision.

You must be willing to take a risk to get to the true objection. If you don't think the sale will be made anyway, take more risk. Use *tough sales* or *no sales* as learning experiences. See how far you can go to get the truth.

The real truths hurt. Are you ready for all six of them?

1. **You haven't created enough need.**

2. **You haven't uncovered the real objection.**

3. **You haven't created enough urgency.**

4. **You haven't convinced the prospect of the benefits of ownership.**

5. **You haven't built enough trust.**

6. **You haven't built enough confidence. Have you?**

What *not to do* and what *to do:*

- **Don't blame it on the prospect.**

- **Don't moan about what the prospect's excuse is.**

- **Figure out what the true objection is.**

- **Figure out a solution for that objection.**

- **Try your best to overcome it to make the sale this time.**

- **AND be sure you prevent that objection from recurring the next time.**

The burden is on you. If you want to sell professionally, get real about who is at fault when a sale isn't made.

When the sale is over and you have lost, be willing to accept the responsibility for the process, hold your head high, and move on to help the next prospect.

Get a mirror. Get responsible. Get your way.

"On the other hand, you need to know when to let go of a bad idea."

Free Git𝕏Bit...**Want to know the seven steps to overcoming an objection and the perfect response when the customer says, "I want to think it over"?** Go to www.gitomer.com, register if you are a first-time user, and enter the word OBJECTION in the GitBit box.

Failed to get your way? No, failed to establish confidence!

7

The prospect said NO! Rats.

Did you lose the sale or just fail to make it? You're sure that prospect should have bought. As you head back to the car, licking your wounds, you try to justify or figure out why the prospect turned you down.

Once you've answered the fundamental questions of self-doubt – was I enthusiastic, friendly, and professional looking – you may have to dig a bit deeper for the true answers. Even though the truth hurts, realizing what you failed to do is a big step in getting your way next time.

Let me give you AND save you some anguish: *You failed to establish buyer confidence, Sparky.* "Hey, Jeffrey, you're dead wrong. That guy really liked me," you say. Maybe. But likability is only one part of the sales equation.

Take the *Jeffrey Gitomer Establish Confidence Test* and rate your ability. If you're willing to be objective about yourself and your abilities, ask yourself the following 14.5 revealing questions and rate yourself, 1 through 10, on each question. (1 is worst, 10 is best.)

1. Was I on time? Did I show up five minutes early (good) or five minutes late (real bad)?

2. Was I prepared? Did I walk into my appointment with everything I needed to make the sale?

3. Was I organized? Did I have everything at my fingertips or was I fumbling?

4. Could I answer all product questions? Do I really have command of my product, or am I constantly having to "get back to you on that one?"

5. Did I make excuses or blame others about anything? The sample wasn't shipped on time... The company didn't send the right information...

6. Was I apologizing? "Sorry I'm late, unprepared, don't know the answer, didn't bring the correct information, and quoted the wrong price."

7. Did the prospect probe personal issues about my company? "If I buy," says Mr. Johnson, "how do I know you'll be here to service me in six months?"

8. Did the prospect ask doubting questions about my product? "What happens if it breaks down after the warranty?" or "Who else buys this product?"

9. Did the prospect ask doubting questions about me? "How long have you been with the company?" or "How much experience do you have?"

10. Did I name-drop other happy, loyal customers effectively?
Or did I fail to use the name of a happy customer to answer a pointed question?

11. Did I feel as though I was on the defensive? Was I constantly answering questions dealing in subject matter other than my product/service? Could I prove my points?

12. Could I overcome all objections in a confident manner?
Did I find myself unable to respond confidently about price, quality, and other issues blocking the sale when asked by the prospect? Did I try to fake it?

13. Did I down the competition? Did I berate my competitor (possibly the prospect's supplier)? Did I make disparaging remarks about the competition to try to make me or my product look better?

14. Was my prospect uninvolved in the sales presentation?
Did the prospect just sit there or, worse, do other things while I was talking?

14.5 Was I too anxious to make the sale? Was it obvious to the prospect there was a commission involved?

Tough questions. But I ask them because "confidence" is elusive, tough to establish, and easily lost at the beginning of any relationship. These questions are designed for you to evaluate your sales performance and reveal your ability (or inability) to create prospect confidence from someone who just said no. The answers will lead you to the next sale, better prepared to make it through confidence rather than through manipulation.

One of the primary lessons of sales is *if they like you, believe you, trust you, and have confidence in you, they MAY buy from you*. If any of those four elements are missing, the answer changes from sale to no sale.

When the prospect says "NO," it's most likely a vote of no confidence. Double rats!

"For 35 years, I tried to sign you up as a client. Now that we're both here, I've got the rest of eternity to keep trying!"

Free Git✗Bit: **Want my list of 10.5 rules that are at the core of your ability to understand and deal with the prospect?** Go to www.gitomer.com, register if you are a first-time user, and enter the words POINT OF VIEW in the GitBit box.

Expose yourself to no and not now to get to yes

97% of all sales are *not* made on the first call.

7

It takes between five and ten exposures (follow-ups) for a prospect to say "yes." The prospect may not actually say "no" each time, but each time you follow up and the prospect doesn't buy, he's saying "Not now, buddy. Do something else for me. I'm still shopping around. I haven't met with my partner. Try again later." In short, "You haven't sold me yet."

As a professional salesperson, you better have what it takes to persevere through the follow-up process and not quit. Be willing to put forth the (creative, value-driven) effort to get to the last no, or consider taking a job in a warehouse with an hourly salary.

Here are follow-up guidelines to ensure closing success:

- **Know the real reasons your prospect wants and needs your product.**

- **Know the real reasons your prospect does not want or need your product.**

- **Be friendly. People like to buy from friends.**

- Know your prospect's hot buttons (things you believe will make the prospect buy), and work with them in constructing your follow-up plan.

- Talk about how your product is used. Know how your customer will produce more. And know how your customer will profit more as a result of owning your product.

- Present new information relative to the sale each time you call or visit.

- Be sincere about your desire to help the customer first and earn the commission second.

- Be direct in your communication. Beating around the bush will only frustrate the prospect (and probably cause him to buy elsewhere). Answer all questions. Don't patronize the prospect.

- Use humor. Be funny. People love to laugh. Making your prospect laugh is a great way to establish common ground and rapport.

- When in doubt, sell the prospect for their reasons, not yours.

- Don't be afraid to ask for the sale each time.

BIG HINT: No perceived difference, no sale. **BIGGER HINT:** No perceived value, no sale. **BIGGEST HINT:** If you are calling and not leaving a message, it's because you have nothing of value to say.

If there was a formula for following up, it would be their reasons + new information + perceived difference + value + their profit + productivity + creative + sincere + direct + friendly + humor + ask = SALE.

But there isn't an exact formula. Every follow-up is different, and elements from the above guidelines must be chosen as called for.

Here are a few lead-in lines you might try so that you don't feel uneasy about how to start the conversation:

- **I discovered something that I believe to be an important factor in your decision...**

- **I just e-mailed you a letter from a customer who had an experience like yours...**

- **Something new has occurred that I thought you would like to know about...**

- **I was thinking about you and called to see if you found out about...**

DON'T SAY: "I called to see if you got my letter, proposal, info, or sample." It sounds dumb, and it gives the prospect a way out. If he doesn't want to talk to you he'll say, "No, I never got it." Where does that leave you? Nowhere.

WHY NOT TRY: "I sent you some (name the stuff) the other day and I wanted to go over a couple of things with you personally because they weren't self-explanatory."

Some salespeople fear that they're "bugging" the prospect if they call too often. If you feel that way, it's for 2.5 reasons:

1. **You haven't established enough rapport and have limited access.**

2. **Your follow-ups are about selling (your money) and not about helping (their value).**

2.5 **You lack the belief in your company, your product, or worse – yourself.**

It's likely you are bugging the prospect if you call more than three times without a returned call, if you ask dumb or pushy questions (you didn't listen well in the first place, or your quota is at the deadline), if you are perceived as insincere, if you exert pressure too soon or too often, or if you are in any way rude to the prospect or anyone on his staff.

It's likely you won't bug the prospect if you have something new, creative, or funny to say, if you're short and to the point, if he considers what you have to be valuable to him, if he's genuinely interested in your product or service, or if he likes you.

If you are creative, helpful, and sincere in your follow-ups, the prospect will not perceive you as a "sales hound."

Follow-up is another word for sale. Your ability to follow up will determine your success in sales. Ask any professional salesperson the secret for success and they will answer "persistence."

The hot-air factor. How full of it are you?

Getting your way requires self-confidence. But there's a fine line between self-confidence and cockiness. And a finer line between self-assurance and arrogance.

The finest line is the one between proud and egotistical.

As a professional salesperson, there's a career of difference between *self-talk = self-performance* (the right way) and *loose lips sink ships* (the ultra-wrong way).

Salespeople are not the most loved group of professionals to begin with. They rank above politicians, tax collectors, and (especially) lawyers, but below dentists and dog catchers. All that salespeople can hope to do is establish a great reputation and let that propel them to success.

Because the prospect buys the salesperson first, reputation is as valuable (and critical) an element as he or she can have. How is yours?

One bad event, situation, or story can ruin years of hard work. Continuing stories of neglect or overpromising breed career destruction. A salesperson's self-delusion (failure to admit the problem and thinking nothing is wrong) will make the situation worse.

Sales hot air can occur at any level. Customers, prospects, bosses, and co-workers are all potential victims.

"Come on, Jeffrey," you say. "Get to the point. Give me some examples of self-destructive talk. What is 'sales hot air?'" Relax helium breath, here 'tiz.

Here are 7.5 examples of hot air (even though I'm sure none of these apply to you):

1. BTNA. Big talk, no action. Too much time talking about the sales you're going to make and not enough time making them.

2. Bragging too soon. Before the deal is signed, sealed, and a check delivered.

3. Bragging too much. No one but you wants to hear it. If you really need to hear yourself, just make a tape of yourself and replay it in your car until *you* get as sick of it as others.

4. Bragging at the expense of others. Beat the competition, but don't beat them into the ground. A variation of this is making someone else look like a fool – bragging about someone you took advantage of or tricked.

5. Using others as scapegoats to get yourself off the hook. Better known as covering your butt, or the inability to accept responsibility. Blaming others for your failings is obvious to those listening, and makes a fool out of the teller (you).

6. Exaggerating the facts. Each year, the fish that got away increases in size. Stay within the parameters of what you know to be true – or less. Understated is always better.

7. Using insincere words. *Honestly, truthfully, quite frankly,* and *I mean that* are words that alienate.

7.5 Talking past the sale. Know when to shut up and go home. Employing any one of the above elements after a sale has been consummated – but before you leave – will jeopardize the sale. It's known as "buying it back" and it happens often. The rule of thumb in sales is "less is more."

Hot air has interesting negative side effects...

- **It wastes everyone's time.**

- **It's the most unproductive and negative use of your time possible.**

- **It makes you look like a fool.**

- **It lowers your respect factor by 100.**

- **It gets people talking behind your back.**

- **It prevents advancement.**

- **It can get you fired.**

Who wants that? No one! But these side effects are linked to people with severe cases of hot air.

How do you know if this is you? How do you know if you're blowing hot air? Well, no one is without *some* guilt.

It's hard not to brag if you just made a big sale and took it out from under the nose of your biggest competitor.

The rules are simple:

- **Don't say anything behind anyone's back you wouldn't say to their face.**

- **Don't say something you wouldn't want said about you.**

- **Don't say anything you have to remember. (Lies must be remembered, or you get tripped up with the truth.)**

- **Don't say anything you couldn't or wouldn't say in front of your mother.**

SECRET: Temper your remarks with humility.

Your challenge is to always bring out the good side in your words. Your challenge is to employ self-discipline in getting past hot air. Your challenge is to self-rule or self-destruct. If you want to get your way, and get it again, leave the hot air out of your language.

Free speech – the legacy you leave to yourself

Want 50 new leads a week?

HERE'S HOW: Give a free speech at a civic group.

Many salespeople are looking to emerge and are frantically trying to "market" themselves with brochures, direct mail, cold calling, and networking. Expensive frustration.

The best way to market yourself is give yourself to the market.

Expose yourself to your prospects.

My advice: Free speech.

Or, to put it a bit clearer, speak for free. Free speech pays. Big pay. And free speech has rewards. Big rewards.

NOTE WELL: I said "speech" not "sales pitch."

When you show up at a civic organization to deliver a free, 15-20 minute talk, here's the gold you receive:

- **You get to give a live sales performance to sell YOURSELF, not your product or service.**

- **You get to do an audition – right in front of the decision maker.**

- **You build (and strengthen) your network.**

- **You (re)establish your presence.**

- **You help the community.**

- **You build your speaking skills, your performance skills, and your storytelling skills.**

- **You get to try out new material.**

- **You will attract new customers (all leaders).**

- **If you're just starting out in your business, you'll have a great opportunity to move up the ladder.**

- **You transfer helpful knowledge to the audience.**

- **You get a chance to have meaningful impact on someone through your words.**

- **You eat for free.**

Now, to some of the above "rewards" you may want to add the prefix phrase "if you're great" to get the real meaning and make the most impact – but I think the message is clear.

Want the best strategy of approach?

Here are the 6.5 success tactics of giving a free speech:

1. Don't give a sales pitch, but do speak on your topic. If you sell burglar alarms, speak about home safety. If you sell copiers, speak about image and office productivity. Get it?

2. Pick a great audience. There are groups and there are more groups – pick the best ones (highest profile, most likely to have the bigwigs).

3. Give a handout. Even if it's just a few pages, a handout will help the audience follow along. It precludes you from having to memorize the talk and gives each member of the audience a way to contact you. WARNING: Give out the handout when you *start* to use it, *never before you begin*. If you give out the handout before you start your talk, people will read one thing while you're speaking about another and (worse) you'll lose audience control and the impact of your message.

4. Videotape it. After the talk you can play the video at home and see how good you *really* are as opposed to how good you *think* you are.

5. Ask for audience evaluations. Ask for positive responses. What they liked best and a candid comment.

6. Give value, get leads. At the end of your talk, offer something additional for free in exchange for their card. The cards you get are *leads*.

6.5 Hang around after the meeting. That's when you find out what your impact was and who your best prospects are.

SECRET: Don't sell your stuff at the meeting. Make a lunch appointment or breakfast meeting, and avoid making a sales pitch or bragging about your company.

On a personal note, this is how I got started getting paid to speak. As a result of my weekly column in the paper, several Rotary and Kiwanis clubs in town called me to give a talk. I decided *not* to talk on sales (my expertise). Rather, I spoke about children (my favorite topic) and titled the talk, "What we've learned from our kids."

I selected seven skills my kids had helped me strengthen in the rearing process (like imagination, persistence, blind faith, enthusiasm) and told a brief story about each. In twenty minutes, I made the audience laugh, cry, think, and learn.

I had a handout and also offered the seven best parenting rules I'd ever learned (for free) if they would just give me their card. At the end of every meeting, I *always* had at least 50 cards and one *paid* talk from someone who said, "How'd you like to come speak to my employees?"

So, my rewards (and yours) for giving a free 20-minute talk included a live audition and sales call in front of 100 decision makers, audience impact, new friends, a self-taught lesson, a practice session, a free lunch, a pen (their usual gift for the talk), a certificate of thanks from the group, 50 warm leads, and a paid engagement.

BONUS TIP: Any group will pay you $100 if you have them make the check out to your favorite charity in your name and theirs.

Interested? Just contact any civic organization in your city. They are dying for a good talk. Every week, they go looking for *good* speakers. And it sure beats cold calling.

"You've been shaking my hand for six minutes, said my name 19 times in a single sentence, and mirrored every gesture I've made including the nose pick I did just to test you. I'm guessing you're here to sell me something."

No matter who you are or where you are in your sales career, free speech can impact learning and earning. Free speech isn't just a right – it's an opportunity. Exercise yours.

– Jeffrey Gitomer

28.5 elements of the greatest sales presentation in the world

7

No two sales presentations are alike, even if you're selling the same product and work for the same company.

Making a presentation is delicate, even if you're selling 18-wheel trucks. Making a memorable presentation is complex, even if you're selling paper clips. Your entire sale rests on words, attitudes, and perceptions.

Everyone has a different *style* of selling – but the *elements of content and process* in a presentation must be the same. You master the elements and then adapt them to your style. It's *what you say* (the elements) combined with *how you say it* (your style).

Here are the 28.5 strategic elements of "what you say":

1. Get to the purpose of your visit right away. "My objective today is…" State it as succinctly as possible. The prospect wants to know your motive for being in his office. The sooner you state it, the clearer (and more relaxed) the atmosphere will be. After the purpose is stated, you can digress to personal issues and rapport building.

2. Say it in terms of how you help, not a bunch of boring facts about why your product works. Tell prospects things about how your product or service solves problems and works on the job, or how your product or service works to serve *their* customers. People don't care what you do – unless what you do benefits them. Start with the attitude, "I'm here to help," not "I'm here to sell."

3. Be the happiest, most positive, most enthusiastic person on the face of the earth. Happiness and enthusiasm are contagious (and attractive). A happy atmosphere is a buying atmosphere. Let your desire to help shine the strongest.

4. Get friendly and comfortable before you begin. Don't start selling without a warm-up. Establish rapport, or no sale. If they don't like you or trust you, they won't buy from you – no matter what. Get personal information. Use it for reference. Link it to the prospect and the order.

5. Build confidence, trust, and credibility. People want someone who can get the job done. Gain confidence.

6. Use power phrases and buzzwords in your industry. The right language gives the prospect confidence that you understand the product – and his business. Powerful phrases send the message that buying is safe and secure.

7. Tell "why we're different," instead of "who we are." If a prospect is buying a copier, he thinks they're all the same. Don't use the word competition. Substitute the words "industry standard" instead. Get creative, not dirty.

8. Say everything in terms of *you* and *your*, not *me*, *I*, or *we*. Language syntax sets a tone for the sale. Be sure the tone you set is one that appears to take the perspective of the only person that matters – the prospect. Talking in terms of "you" automatically sets that tone.

9. Ask intelligent questions. Identifying needs, getting important information, creating interest, gaining confidence, qualifying affordability, establishing credibility, and closing the sale all stem from asking questions. Integral (power) questions must be preplanned and prewritten for maximum benefit. Any questions?

10. Identify personal goals and business goals. You strengthen your ability to build a real relationship by identifying both. Often, there is a link.

11. Find out any past bad or good concerning your product or service. This line of questioning will bring about real needs, desires, and concerns before you get into your actual presentation.

12. Focus on the value of what you offer and how that value meets his/her needs. Forget about price – the prospect will five minutes after he becomes a customer and something goes wrong. Concentrate on value and productive use of the product.

13. Focus your talk on their profit, their productivity, and how they will use your product to make this happen. When you talk about these elements, it makes your prospect perceive ownership. You talk about these elements as though your potential buyer has already taken possession.

14. Move quickly through your presentation, but be sure you're understood. Don't assume the prospect knows what you *should* have said. Your prospect is hearing this for the first time (even though it might be *your* 1,000th). Cover every basic aspect of your presentation. Balance that with the fact that our society is getting less patient.

15. Take notes constantly. This element sounds too obvious to be mentioned, but I'm amazed at how few salespeople take notes. Taking notes says, "I'm interested in you, and what you have to say is important." It also gives you the notes to make perfect follow-ups and accurate deliveries.

16. Involve the prospect. Test him. Let him do the demonstration. The sooner you gain involvement, the easier it is to gain prospect understanding and confidence. Let him help you set up. Letting them touch the product creates an early sense of ownership.

17. Take it back. Keep control at all times. If you give samples or literature to the prospect, don't continue until they have looked, touched, or read – and then ask for them (take them) back. It's your presentation – keep total control of it. Make the prospect pay attention to you – not your samples or papers. **NOTE:** If they ask to see again what you took away, it's a big, perhaps a closing, buying signal.

18. Use testimonials when the time is right. They are the only proof you've got. Use them to overcome doubts, objections, stalls, or specific issues that are blocking the sale.

19. To gain understanding, ask approval questions. Getting approvals along the way leads to getting approval at the end. Questions like "Don't you agree?" or "Do you understand how this helps?" Or shorter versions such as "Isn't it?" and "Doesn't it?" set a tone of yes in the mind of the prospect throughout the presentation.

20. Make the prospect qualify, too. You want to do business with the people most likely to help you grow and prosper. Ninety-five percent of your headaches and complaints come from five percent of your customers. Retrain them, or fire them. **NOTE OF CAUTION:** You may be selling them wrong and creating your own problems.

21. Learn to recognize buying signals. Usually revealed in the form of a question about price, delivery, specific features, or productivity. Close when you hear them. Don't answer with "Yes" or "No." If you do, you'll go past the sale.

22. Overcome objections before they occur. I don't care what product or service you sell. There are only ten major objections a prospect can raise, and you've heard them all before. Wake up – anticipate them and address them in your presentation before the prospect has a chance to raise them.

23. Sell timely payment for your product or services rendered. Don't make half a sale. *Sell how and when payment is expected.* It's incredible to me how many salespeople are afraid of asking for the money.

24. Don't close the sale – Assume the sale. Assume it from the moment you enter the room. Then, take the logical steps to complete the transaction. The sale is a given if the need is present and the presentation is superior.

25. Close the sale completely. Handle the details and confirm the next action. State what you need to get started. Make an appointment to review and begin. Handle the last detail between when the prospect says yes and when ownership is taken.

26. Be bold. For fun, I try (without asking) to get the buyer to stand and walk around (I walk around first). Then I sit in *his* chair at *his* desk. I get a surprised look, most times a laugh or smile, and have never had a negative response. You can't do it to everyone – but I dare you to try it once.

27. Be incredible. Create an attraction to you through superior presentation skills, product knowledge, and the ability to meet the prospect's needs. Make the prospect feel that buying anyplace else would be the biggest mistake of his life.

28. Strive for long-term relationships with everyone. When you do this, you automatically eliminate any greed or short-term thinking from the sale. You will always be thinking "what is best for this prospect" not "what is best for me." If you think "long term," it will result in "big sale."

28.5 Be funny and have fun. Most people have no fun at work. If you're fun and funny, you'll have an attraction and an advantage. "Make me laugh, and you can make me buy" is a credo you can take to the bank. Laughing all the way.

These 28.5 elements can only be looked at as a whole while you're in the presentation itself. To get great at the sales presentation process, you must be great at each individual element.

Making a simple presentation is a complex issue. It's a far cry from telling a bunch of facts about your product or service. Product knowledge is the easy part – a given before you make a sales call.

A sale is always made. Either you sell the prospect on "yes" or they sell you on "no."

Want one tip that ties the whole process together? Approach each element from the customer's perspective – it's the only one that matters.

WORDS OF CAUTION: Some people may just be selling for the money. They will be smelled out in a minute. They shall be know as "Phoenicians." (It's been shortened to phonies over the years.)

Don't do it for the money; do it because you believe it passionately. Do it because you love it.

Free Git✗Bit...If you don't believe it and if you don't love it, it may be because you haven't discovered your why. To discover, go to www.gitomer.com, register if you are first-time user, and enter the words MY WHY in the GitBit box.

ELEMENT

8

THE WRITE WAY TO GET YOUR WAY

"I have writer's block."

"Is it writer's block? Or you're just a block head?"

What makes writing persuasive?

Writing becomes persuasive when others are willing to act on, or comment on, what you've written.

Interestingly, people will write to me and say, "I agree 100%," while others will say, "I disagree 100%." Same article – it just strikes people a different way. Your goal in persuasive writing is to strike a nerve but not to polarize.

I wrote a very controversial piece on noncompete clauses. It brought hundreds of responses from out of the woodwork. Personally, I am against noncompete clauses. So are 100% of the salespeople who responded to the article. Their bosses, however, saw it a different way. They were looking to place golden handcuffs, protect their best interest, and, in short, exercise their paranoia that a salesperson would run away to the competition and steal the company's customers.

And, by the way, that's not persuasion. Getting someone to sign a noncompete clause is not persuasion – it's intimidation.

Persuasion comes from taking a stand and being adamant about it, proving points about it, and asking questions about it to make the reader or listener think and act.

Persuasive writing is also succinct. It gets to the point right away. It talks about how the other person is affected more than it talks about what you do. You can use examples, but they have to be compelling. And they have to make the reader shake his head "yes."

Every week, I write a column on sales, customer service, customer loyalty, or personal development. At the bottom of the column, there's a directive to go to my Web site and get additional information for no cost. Thousands of people go there each day because they believe that they will gain additional benefit – and they're right.

Free Git✗Bit... Right now, go to www.gitomer.com, register if you're a first-time user, and enter the word NONCOMPETE in the GitBit box. You'll get the controversial article I wrote on noncompete clauses.

8

Persuasive writing prevails when the reader makes a photocopy and gives it to someone else, sends an e-mail with "Hey, you gotta read this," or is persuaded to take an action as a result of reading.

Look at the common brochure. Every company has one. It's called a "marketing piece" or sometimes "company literature." I call them "wastes of money."

Have you ever read a persuasive brochure? A value-based brochure? If you have, it's been less than 1/10,000. The Harvard Business Review would write an article on "The New Face of Corporate Literature."

HERE'S THE CLUE: Think about everything you write in terms of its impact – not just its information.

ASK YOURSELF: Will this compel someone to take action? If it doesn't, then you have to rewrite it until it does. Even something so simple as a self-test or getting someone's opinion will create actionable words and a greater chance for persuasion or a response to occur.

TEST YOURSELF: Read all of your writings. If you received them in the mail, would you keep them, or throw them away? If you saw them in print, would you read them and take action, or would you skip them?

Whatever you would do, it's likely that the people you seek to influence, the people you seek to persuade, will do the same.

I love when companies brag "made with recycled paper" on their brochure. *Hello! It's recycled from your last crappy brochure that everybody threw away.*

THINK "VALUE FOR THEM": Create a brochure or a document that talks about five ways to benefit from, or five ways to profit from, or five ways to produce more from whatever it is that you're selling. That's a piece of literature that your customers are likely to keep forever.

RED PEN YOURSELF: Get a red Sharpie pen and gather all your corporate literature. As you read your own self-serving stuff, circle anything that you are certain your customer will want to keep or show to others. It's likely that you will never remove the cap from the pen.

While this is a painful exercise, it's also the reality of how your customer views your literature.

For writing to be both powerful and compelling, it's up to you!

Over the past 15 years, I have become a successful writer. Many of you aspire to do the same – or at least to become a *better* writer.

I get requests for help every day. People ask, "How can I write like you?" Or they say "I'm not a very good writer" or "I sit down to write and nothing comes out."

8

I cannot teach you "how to write" or "how to write better." But I can share with you *how I write*, and you can take it from there.

Here are my realities of writing that may help you on your path to becoming a better writer:

I WRITE LIKE I THINK. I WRITE LIKE I TALK. The thoughts I write are a silent extension of what I would have said if I were speaking aloud. That's why I read aloud when I edit. I want my writing to sound like I'm talking. I will often get a letter or e-mail that says, "I felt like you were talking to me as I was reading" or "I felt like you were standing right there." That's because I "write" in "speak."

I WRITE ANYWHERE, ANYTIME. I don't need a space or a place. I just need an idea or a thought. I write when an idea strikes. If I'm not near a computer, I find any scrap of paper or napkin I can get my hands on. The object is to capture the idea or thought the moment it pops into your mind. You will *never* remember it later.

I COLLECT IDEAS. I COLLECT THOUGHTS. I have hundreds of them. When I want to write about something or I have a deadline, I select one of my ideas and expand on it.

WHEN I GET THE IDEA, I STRETCH IT. I write everything that comes to mind. All of the thoughts, phrases, or words I can think of. I just brain dump until it's all out. I may edit a few things when I'm done, but I write and dictate in a flurry because ideas are fleeting and thoughts are even more fleeting. In 15 years of writing, the one thing I have found to be most true is that thoughts will leave your head if you don't write them down at once.

8

I WRITE FROM MY OWN EXPERIENCE. I don't need research statistics to back up a thought or a concept. Either it happened to me, or I believe it to be true based on my personal experience. Statistics lie. I don't.

WHEN I WRITE A COLUMN OR A CHAPTER, I STICK TO ONE SUBJECT, THOUGHT, OR THEME. This creates an in-depth look and forces me to look beyond the norm and create new ideas for worn-out methods and conventional thinking.

I WRITE WITH AUTHORITY. I'm emphatic and declarative. If you read my thoughts, you have no doubt about what I'm saying or how I feel about it.

I DON'T "CALL IT" ANYTHING. If it's common, don't claim ownership. I'll be reading a story or a chapter in someone else's book, and the writer will say, "And I call that customer service." *Well, hey there, Sparky. What does everyone else call it?* It's a million times more powerful and authoritative to say, "It's called: customer service."

I DON'T CARE ABOUT GRAMMAR. I write so that the reader can "get it." I care about how it sounds when it's read and how it looks when you read it, not what some silly rule says. I put hyphens and apostrophes where they don't belong, so the reader has an easy time following the flow and understanding the thought.

I CARE ABOUT STRUCTURE AND FLOW. I want one thought to flow to another. Where it doesn't or can't, I make (structure) a list of things. The lists flow from top to bottom.

I RELY ON SPELL CHECKER AND KEEP ON WRITING UNTIL I COMPLETE THE THOUGHT. I never stop writing to "fix" something until the thought I'm writing is complete. Spelling and writing are mutually exclusive. If you stop to spell, you lose thought flow and momentum. You can always check your spelling; you can't always retain the thought or flow.

I WRITE IN THE MALE GENDER BECAUSE I'M A MALE. I never mean to offend anyone. I'm trying to make points, generate new thinking, and help people succeed. That advice knows no gender. Read *between* the pronouns. Don't get hung up on them.

MY WRITING VOICE IS NOT PC. If I waste time with "his or her," I lose my thought. I don't mean to be insulting. I'm just writing in my voice. It's how I grew up. It's the same voice as all the early books I read, and continue to read. **NOTE WELL:** It's a *message* and a *thought*; it's an *idea* or a *strategy* – not a gender.

I DO NOT INCLUDE MYSELF WITH THE READER. I separate myself from the reader with pronouns. I say "you," "your," "they," "he," "she," "it," or "the." NEVER "we" or "our." I talk to the reader, but never include myself in the thought. NOT, "We all know…" rather, "You know." NOT, "Our thoughts tell us…" rather, "Your thoughts tell you…"

I BREAK THE RULES OF TRADITIONAL WRITING, GRAMMAR, AND PUNCTUATION. Teachers of grammar would not give me a passing grade. I could care less. I've sold a million books. How many have they sold?

8

I EDIT WHEN I FINISH, BUT I EDIT BETTER A DAY LATER. Editing is revealing. It tells you what you were thinking at the moment you wrote it. Editing a day later reveals, "What was I thinking when I wrote this?" My editing secret is that I read aloud when I edit. And I ask others to edit when I think I'm finished. Both of these secrets make my writing twice as powerful.

Free Git𝄞Bit...Looking for someone to polish your work and make it BEST? To read a list of 20.5 things to look for in an editor, written by my personal editor, Jessica McDougall, go to www.gitomer.com, register if you are first-time user, and enter the word EDITOR in the GitBit box.

I END MY LISTS WITH .5 RATHER THAN A WHOLE NUMBER, FOR 2.5 BASIC REASONS:

1. The .5 statement at the end of each list I make is the glue that binds the rest of the list.

2. Ending this way makes me think deeper about the subject. Think of a higher level. Here's where I can add philosophy, humor, challenge, and a final call to action.

2.5 It makes my lists different from all other lists. It brands me and sets me apart from all other list makers (except for the few that copy me).

8 **I USE FIRST PERSON SINGULAR SPARINGLY.** If you're familiar with my writing, you know I avoid first person plural (we, our) like the plague. It sucks the power out of writing and it drains the impact by lowering the value of the writer. When you write, you are the authority – the reader is not. Don't include yourself with them.

I LOVE TO WRITE. This may be the biggest secret of writing with passion and clarity. I believe loving it makes the thoughts flow deeper and more consistently. I believe loving it makes me consider "long-term legacy" as well as "short-term impact." I believe my love of writing makes me a more complete writer. Content becomes more relevant, and pride of authorship shows through in every sentence.

Writing leads to wealth.

– Jeffrey Gitomer

Less about me, more about your writing skills

Here are 5.5 things you can do to improve your skills today:

1. **Just sit down and write something.** Every day. Pick a topic or pick something that happened to you that you would like to clarify or get off your chest. Writing clarifies thinking. It also creates freedom for additional thought. When the idea is down on paper, it no longer clutters your mind. It's the same with thoughts – the same with stories. Writing memorializes, clarifies, and clears at the same time.

2. **Capture your best thoughts and ideas the second they occur.** When you get an idea, one thought tends to lead to another. They come quickly and they exit just as quickly. The faster you capture, the more complete the idea will be. Write the idea(s) down on anything, but always be ready to transfer the thoughts onto a computer. This will allow you to reread, edit, expand, and preserve your thoughts forever.

3. **Write it like you would say it.** Speak into your computer and speak to yourself as you write the words down – this will help you write a clearer and more complete thought. Many people fight with their words. If you write like you speak, you'll never be "at a loss for words." You'll also never suffer from the myth known as "writer's block."

4. **Make sure your thoughts are simple, easy to understand, and complete.** As you're writing, make certain that you put down everything that is on your mind, and when you're editing or rereading, read it as though it were a story that you would not have to explain to anyone if they were reading it.

5. **Edit early and often.** The moment you finish writing, sit back and reread what you wrote top to bottom. Errors will be apparent. After you finish the first edit, let your writing sit for at least a day. After you've edited your own piece twice, give it to someone you like or trust – someone who will give you objective, honest feedback. Editing will also lead you to additional thoughts.

5.5 **You're writing for the reader AND yourself.** As you edit, read your work as though it was meant for you to read. If you like it, it is likely others will like it. But the true feelings of others will come from their comments. After you've completed outside editing, solicit a dozen people for outside reading. Their comments will determine your fate, or at least the fate of the piece you wrote. The secret is keeping your writing conversational so that when others read it they will feel as though you are talking to them.

Free Git人Bit...**Want 2.5 more ideas on writing that will help you get better at the skill?** Go to www.gitomer.com, register if you're a first-time user, and enter the words WRITE BETTER in the GitBit box.

Proposal...or winning proposal?

Why do you lose more proposals than you win?

The sad reason most companies lose on the proposals they write is that they aren't persuasive. They're just informative, fluffy, and create no compelling reason to act. In short, they're boring, they're losers – and you blame "price."

The skill of drafting *persuasive words* on a proposal is an integral part of the winning process. Some people have a hard time coming up with the appropriate words. Not because they can't write, but because they don't know the rules of writing.

Here are 15.5 writing rules and guidelines to help turn your proposals into winning proposals:

1. Use a headline above the body of text to state your objective.

2. Use short paragraphs. For emphasis.

3. Edit, ~~edit, edit.~~ Take out every word not integral to the purpose or objective of the communication. Avoid heavy syrup. Half the adjectives, half the prepositional phrases, and most adverbs can be eliminated. Look behind commas to see if the entire phrase is worthy of keeping – usually it's not.

4. Keep the proposal short. The shorter it is, the better chance you have of the proposal being read and understood.

5. • **Use bullets to break up the monotony.** They make the proposal easy to read graphically.

   • **Use bullets to make the proposal seem (or be) short and sweet.** Full of meat.

   • **Use bullets to emphasize the most important points.** Indent them for impact.

6. Bold stuff to get attention. But only when it's absolutely necessary. Lead-in words that benefit the reader (buyer) are often the best choice.

7. Don't bold your name. **Bold what is important to the reader.** Your name is among the least important words in the proposal.

8. Edit out (almost) all words that end in "ly."

9. Avoid superlatives ("est").

10. Avoid the word "unique."

11. Don't make it sound like a rubber stamp.

12. Don't misspell a word. One man misspelled "potato" and he paid for it dearly, perhaps for a career. Luckily, he didn't have a very important job.

13. Include the extra – the unexpected – the plus one. Enclose an article or something pertaining to the reader. Something that makes the reader think you went beyond the norm to serve, communicate, and provide value to them.

8

14. Write a great (short and sweet) cover letter.

- Don't make the prospect vomit when he reads your cover letter. Make the letter easy to digest.

- Keep it to one page.

- Don't say "Thank you for the opportunity." Instead, try "We are (I am) proud to offer."

- Don't resell your product – sell the next action step and build confidence and rapport. Don't use the letter as a sales pitch. Use it as a sales tool.

- Never say, "Again, thanks." It's not necessary to thank anyone again. Once is enough. Twice is groveling.

- Ask for a response by a certain date.

- Use a friendly, but professional, closing. "Thank you for your time and consideration. I'll call you Tuesday."

- Sign your first name only. It's more friendly.

15. Read out loud to edit. It's the single MOST POWERFUL editing tool I've ever used.

15.5 It must read like a book. It has to tell your story and sell your story. It needs to speak for you without you being there. It needs to be a winner.

NOTE WELL: Most people don't read the entire proposal. They're just looking for the price. Put your best stuff on the price page.

I learned how to write from my dad and my brother

GUIDELINES (not rules) FOR WRITING RIGHT:

- Learn to write by reading good writers.
- Learn to write by practicing.
- Learn to write by editing a day later.
- Learn to write by establishing a structure.
- Learn to write by understanding that factual, listed content is powerful.
- Adverbs, prepositional phrases, and "est" are out.
- What's the tone? Mine is straightforward and succinct. Mine is real world and humorous.
- What's the voice or author? Mine is authoritative.
- There's power of authority in pronouns. First person, second person, third person.
- He or she? No.
- Use writer's privilege – write in vernacular, not grammar – using incorrect syntax, ain't, gonna.
- Grammar – okay sometimes. For me, it's write like you speak.

8

- Research vs. knowledge. Proof vs. opinion. I use knowledge and opinion.

- Use graphic, alliterative word choices such as vomit or puke.

- Paragraph sizes are small.

- Use repeated themes. **BIG SECRET:** and, **Think about this...**

- Use **bold** and CAPS to make points and emphasize words.

- Grab me at the beginning.

- Start with a question or short statement.

- Make me smile, think, or act at the end. End with impact.

- Give me meat in the middle. All meat.

- **BIG SECRET:** Read aloud when you edit. It's how does it sound, NOT how does it read.

ASK YOURSELF:

- Where's the impact?

- Where's the meat?

- Where's the point?

- Where's the hook?

- Is it compelling?

- Will the reader want to read it all?

- Will the reader think as a result of this writing?

- Will the reader act as a result of this writing?

ELEMENT

9

PERSISTENCE

"Hey, didn't I just see you in the last chapter?"

"They keep telling me, 'No.' They keep telling me, 'No,'"

Look to your kid and your cat for persistence clues

Most persuaders give up too easily. They try to persuade, they try to get their way, BUT the other person for one reason or another is not persuaded, and the persuader gives up. Usually after the first or second rebuff.

ENTER: Persistence.

When persuasion is combined with persistence, your percentage of getting your way success will increase in direct proportion with the quality, the impact, and the value of your message.

In sales, persistence is referred to as a follow up. You don't send a proposal and sit back and wait for the phone to ring. You call the person you sent the proposal to in an attempt to move the process along. The problem with persistence, or follow up, is that most people do it for greed, rather than to help.

Persistence is best defined by looking at the actions of a child or a cat. Neither one ever gives up. A child will do everything from begging to tantrum throwing. A child is willing to take corporal punishment to get their way. When you think about it, it's the only way they know. They're doing what comes naturally, unless the parent can do something that will change the behavior.

I recall walking in a mall with my then 5-year-old daughter Rebecca. She looked in a store window and asked, "Dad, can I have that T-shirt?" "Not today," I said, and we kept on walking. After about 100 yards I asked Rebecca, "How come you didn't throw a fit like you do with your mother?" Rebecca offhandedly responded to me and said, "It doesn't work with you, Dad." That was a shock to me, and a lesson.

Now think about your cat. When the cat is hungry, the cat will never give up. The cat will jump on tables, jump on people, make loud noises, and knock things down on purpose. In short, they'll do anything to get fed.

The cat will start out with a gentle meow, maybe rub up against your leg, maybe run to her dish as you begin to walk. But ignoring the cat will only make her persistence meter get to the red line. The meowing gets louder, the running around and jumping gets noisier, things will get knocked down, if she has claws they will begin to dig into you, and she will use every method at her disposal in order to be fed, only saying one word all the while – "Meow!"

Now think about the percentage of victory of your kid and your cat, and you at once realize that persistence pays. The question is *how do you refine yours so that people perceive a value, not a pest?* The secret is allowing the other person to feel a valid reason for your persistence. If they do, they will embrace you rather than avoid you.

The cat will get her way 100% of the time. If you want to learn how to get your way – get a cat.

Once you master persuasion, you have to learn persistence if you really want to get your way.

— Jeffrey Gitomer

Why do some persist and some quit?

Why do people quit too soon? Big question.
Why do you quit to soon? Bigger question.
Have you read *Think and Grow Rich*? Biggest question.

Reason? *Think and Grow Rich* (written by Napoleon Hill over 70 years ago) has an entire chapter on persistence that provides real insight as to the characteristics of what makes some stick at it until they win, while others stop either just after they start, or stop just before they are about to taste victory.

Rather than be so presumptuous as to paraphrase the great Napoleon Hill, I am going to give you the *exact* words of the master. Below in italics are some excerpts (and insights) on persistence quoted exactly as they were written seven decades ago. Here's the best part: They're still applicable today.

Persistence is a state of mind, therefore it can be cultivated. Like all states of mind, persistence is based upon definite causes, among them these:

a. **Definiteness of purpose.** *Knowing what one wants is the first and, perhaps, the most important step toward the development of persistence. A strong motive forces one to surmount many difficulties.*

b. **Desire.** *It's comparatively easy to acquire and to maintain persistence in pursuing the object of intense desire.*

c. **Self-reliance.** *Belief in one's ability to carry out a plan encourages one to follow the plan through with persistence.*

d. **Definiteness of plans.** *Organized plans, even though they may be weak and entirely impractical, encourage persistence.*

e. **Accurate knowledge.** *Knowing that one's plans are sound, based upon experience or observation, encourages persistence; "guessing" instead of "knowing" destroys persistence.*

f. **Cooperation.** *Sympathy, understanding, and harmonious cooperation with others tends to develop persistence.*

g. **Will-power.** *The habit of concentrating one's thoughts upon the building of plans for the attainment of a definiteness of purpose leads to persistence.*

h. **Habit.** *Persistence is the direct result of habit. The mind absorbs and becomes a part of the daily experience upon which it feeds. Fear, the worst of all enemies, can be effectively cured by forced repetition of acts of courage. Everyone who has seen active service in war knows this.*

HOW TO DEVELOP PERSISTENCE.

There are four simple steps which lead to the habit of persistence. They call for no great amount of intelligence, no particular amount of education, and little time or effort.

The necessary steps are:

1. *A definite purpose backed by burning desire for its fulfillment.*

2. *A definite plan, expressed in continuous action.*

3. *A mind closed tightly against all negative and discouraging influences, including negative suggestions of relatives, friends, and acquaintances.*

4. *A friendly alliance with one or more persons who will encourage one to follow through with both plan and purpose.*

These four steps are essential for success in all walks of life. The entire purpose of the principles of the (Think and Grow Rich) *philosophy is to enable one to take these four steps as a matter of habit.*

The secret of persistence is not an answer; it's a realization. And if you read the preceding excerpts and didn't "get it," you will get beat by someone who did.

The Napoleon Hill philosophy of persistence is strong, yet soft. The only omission from the strategy is "what" to persist with. Let me give you that answer in a word – *value.*

"What you need to develop persistence is will-power and desire."

"In other words, how bad do you want it? And how far are you willing to go to get it? Unless the answer is all the way, you will not persist. You will give up."

– Napoleon Hill

Follow-up is another word for persistence

It seems to be a softer word. If a sales manager is talking to a saleperson, he'll never say, "Have you been persistent with the Bigelow account?" Rather, he will say, "Have you followed up with the Bigelow account?"

No different with you. You use some form of persistence in everything that you do. It may be as simple as staying on top of your children to clean their room or do their homework. It may be calling your mortgage lender or banker five times to see if your loan has been approved. It may be to see if you car repair has been done or the insurance company has paid your claim.

Persistence is also a major part of business interaction. Project completion, order shipped on time, arranging a meeting, or simply getting approval from multiple parties.

The way you may know persistence most is from the salesperson who called you repeatedly trying to make the sale. You may have called them a pest. But the main reason they persisted is that you were afraid or embarrassed to tell them no. They wrote notes, they called and left messages – and you refused to respond… and they refused to give up.

Or you may have been the salesperson who made all those futile calls and wrote all those futile notes.

9

Now that I have defined persistence in the obvious way, let me give you a strategy that will help persistence pay, or pay off. The secret lies in your ability to have *something of value* to say when following up or persisting.

Most people persist only to persuade others or get their way. In short, make the sale. The nuance is to engage the other person in thought and provide something of value for them. For them. While you are thinking, "What's in it for me?" the other person is thinking exactly the same thing. Your job as a persuader, your job as a persister, is to provide value to those you seek to sell to, or those you seek to persuade.

Let me define it even further: Many salespeople will follow up a sale by calling the prospect on the phone and saying, "I'm calling to find out if you got the proposal I sent to you two days ago and answer any questions." BIG LIE. You don't care if they have any questions, you just want the money. Why don't you call and say, "I'm calling about the money. Is it ready?" that would be closer to the truth.

OR WORSE: You call to follow up, get voicemail, and hang up without leaving a message. Why?

1. **You have NOTHING OF VALUE to say.**

2. **You have NO RELATIONSHIP.**

2.5 **You're a chicken – scared you'll get rejected.**

HERE'S THE MESSAGE: Persist with value and you will get your way. *Get the message?*

The more you give value, the more you will get your way.

– Jeffrey Gitomer

ELEMENT

ELOQUENCE

9

5

"Hey, how do you like my sweater?"

"It matches your spare tire!"

Is it eloquence or excellence?

I ain't eloquent.

I don't believe if someone is going to describe me as a speaker that they're going to use the word "eloquent." But there are other words that create the aura of eloquence that every speaker must have. Confident. Relaxed. Funny. Engaging. Energetic. Real-word. On-point.

I grew up in New Jersey, but I don't have a discernable "Jersey" accent, predominantly because my mother grew up in Brooklyn and made a conscious effort to change her accent so that it was neutral. And the family was expected to follow suit. This was bad for my brother and me because people from the Northeast tend to be "lazy speakers" who leave off last letters of words and don't enunciate.

At home, every time I said, "Twenney," my mother would raise her voice and say, "Twenty! It's twenty with a T, not twenty with an N!" I hated it then. But it was actually my first speech lesson. My first lesson in eloquence.

Fast forward 45 years. Every time I take the platform, I feel thrilled and privileged that I get to share an information-packed message. For that message to be transferred, a lot of preparation has to take place, both physically and mentally.

.5

Besides being audience-centric, every talk has to be:

- succinct, to the point, fast
- funny without being sarcastic
- humorous at my own expense, not someone else's
- full of stories, not jokes
- them-based, not me-based
- eye-to-eye, not eye-to-audience
- off the platform, not behind the podium
- done in comfortable clothing, in a comfortable setting
- with PowerPoint rather than notes
- with a customized and personalized message
- with good timing and plenty of laughter
- point-based, not me-based
- owned, not memorized

That's eloquence.

To be eloquent, you must tell a story and THEN make a point. Not the other way around. And don't do the old "tell them what you're going to tell them." Just tell them.

Grab your audience at the beginning with thought-provoking words and challenges.

Engage them at the beginning with light-hearted laughter and self-deprecating humor.

.5

Let them know you understand who they are and what they do. Give them answers they can use immediately. Let your words be as genuine as your desire to help. Have one idea that they have never thought of. Deliver it with style. That's eloquence.

Most audience members listening to a speaker for the first time have their arms folded, waiting for proof as to who you are. Most speakers bumble along in the opening thanking people ad nauseum and they lose the audience in one manner or another.

The most common speaker stupidity is entering the platform saying, "Good morning, everyone." The audience meekly replies, "Good morning." The speaker then says, "I SAID GOOD MORNING." The audience screams back, "GOOD MORNING!" The speaker says, "That's more like it," and everyone in the audience hates the speaker for at least the first ten minutes while they try to recover. That's not eloquence, that's arrogance.

I've given over 1,800 speeches in the last 15 years. I have never said "Good morning." I start with a story or a question, and engage the audience in the first ten seconds by making a point and making them laugh. You may not think of that as eloquent, but I can promise you that if you parade in front of them in the finest of clothing and do the "Good Morning" bit, they will perceive you as an elephant in a tu-tu, and you'll spend the next ten minutes dancing out of it.

.5

Eloquence comes from a combination of the way you speak your words clearly and distinctly, and the way you carry yourself as a person – your walk, your swagger, your "way," and the self-confidence you exude as you present your words. It's not a matter of a gesture or a smile. Rather, it's a manner and a style.

The opposite of eloquence is maudlin, sarcastic, cynical, humor at other people's expense, insincere, abuse of first person plural, and other audience manipulative acts like, "You know Sally has worked real hard for this event. Let's all give her a round of applause." Barf.

Eloquence comes from owning your material. Mastering your platform presence. Total control. Nothing fancy.

No big words – but words that count. Words that have meaning. Words that have feeling. And words that are powerful enough to transfer to an audience in a way that they stick and have impact.

If audience members say to themselves, "I get it. I think I can do it. I am willing to try it," then the message has begun to get through. The message has begun to be transferred, and the message has had an impact. That's eloquence.

The reason most messages don't get through is that most presenters (not you, of course) are all wrapped up telling "their story," and have no idea how "their story" might impact the audience.

Eloquence is your ability to create metaphors and examples that transfer the lessons in your message. No one cares about your plight as a speaker, unless they know how it impacts them and how they can get better as a result of it.

> **Eloquence is** delivering your message in terms of the audience.

> **Eloquence is** making sure your message is transferable.

> **Eloquence is** making your message relatable.

> **Eloquence is** customizing and personalizing your message.

> **Eloquence is** enunciating your message.

> **Eloquence is** the audience perceiving that you love what you do.

For me, lessons in eloquence bring memories. Every time I say "twenty" in a talk, I make certain to pronounce the second "t."

It reminds me of my mother in her heavenly home taking pride in her son's eloquence.

.5

I appreciate you

These people have taught me how to get my way, both by telling me "yes" and telling me "no." While the names may mean nothing to you, I challenge you that as you read them – be thinking of the people you need to thank for helping you learn the same process.

If you've noticed, I never dedicate a book to anybody. But please know that every book I write is dedicated to the loving memory of my parents, Max and Florence Gitomer, who during their living years and even thereafter molded my thoughts, helped create my personality and style, and challenged me to become a better person both in love and anger. There's no way to thank them, but the reverence that I have for their lessons is often manifested in the words that I write and speak.

My brother, **JOSH GITOMER**, has re-entered my everyday life. Our friendship and our respect for one another has deepened, and his artistic talent and gentle ways have been a source of help and joy as we mature together.

My friend, my constant companion, my Jiminy Cricket, my editor, and my love, **JESSICA McDOUGALL**, is without peer as a thinker, a creator, and a doer. The serendipity that brought us together has given me happiness, comfort, and a peacefulness of knowing that when all is dark, we share each other's light.

I am the father of many. My daughters **ERIKA**, **STACEY**, and **REBECCA** always got their way. They still do. They were the masters of getting their way until my granddaughters came along.

MORGAN, **JULIA**, and **CLAUDIA** have given new meaning to the words "getting it your way." They don't even have to ask. Somehow, it just happens their way. All my children and grandchildren feel blessed that I am in their lives, but I know the real secret.

MICHAEL WOLFF, fast becoming a member of the Gitomer family, has, with Jessica's guidance, created another piece of legacy. I like Mike because he's a 24/7 guy.

My list of children goes on. There are currently 29 people employed at **BUY GITOMER** and **TRAINONE**. They are not a team – they are a family. I've been an entrepreneur for 50 years in one form or another – but this family is far and away the finest group of people I have ever had the pleasure of working with, or giving them their way.

And **YOU**, the reader…

Thank you for your support in coming to my seminars, buying my books, and being my customer. I appreciate you.

Jeffrey Gitomer
Chief Executive
Salesman

AUTHOR. Jeffrey Gitomer is the author of *The New York Times* best-seller *The Sales Bible, The Little Red Book of Selling, The Little Red Book of Sales Answers, The Little Black Book of Connections,* and *The Little Gold Book of YES! Attitude.* All of his books have been number one best-sellers on Amazon.com including *Customer Satisfaction is Worthless, Customer Loyalty is Priceless* and *The Patterson Principles of Selling.* Jeffrey's books have sold more than a million copies worldwide.

OVER 100 PRESENTATIONS A YEAR. Jeffrey gives public and corporate seminars, runs annual sales meetings, and conducts live and Internet training programs on selling and customer loyalty. He has presented an average of 120 seminars a year for the past 15 years.

IN FRONT OF MILLIONS OF READERS EVERY WEEK. Jeffrey's syndicated column, *Sales Moves,* appears in more than 95 business newspapers worldwide and is read by more than 4 million people every week.

SALES CAFFEINE. Jeffrey's weekly e-zine, *Sales Caffeine,* is a sales wake-up call delivered every Tuesday morning to more than 250,000 subscribers, free of charge. *Sales Caffeine* allows Jeffrey to communicate valuable sales information, strategies, and answers to sales professionals on a timely basis. To subscribe, click on FREE EZINE at www.gitomer.com.

ON THE INTERNET. Jeffrey's WOW! Web sites, www.gitomer.com and www.trainone.com, get as many as 25,000 hits a day from readers and seminar attendees. His state-of-the-art Web presence and e-commerce ability has set the standard among peers, and has won huge praise and acceptance from customers.

TRAINONE ONLINE SALES TRAINING. Online sales training lessons are available at www.trainone.com. The content is pure Jeffrey – fun, pragmatic, real world, and immediately implementable. TrainOne's innovation is leading the way in the field of customized e-learning.

SELLING POWER LIVE. Jeffrey is the host and commentator of *Selling Power Live,* a monthly, subscription-based sales resource bringing together the insights of the world's foremost authorities on selling and personal development.

SALES ASSESSMENT ONLINE. The world's first customized sales assessment, renamed a "successment," will not only judge your selling skill level in 12 critical areas of sales knowledge, but it will also give you a diagnostic report that includes 50 mini sales lessons. This amazing sales tool will rate your sales abilities and explain your customized opportunities for sales knowledge growth. This program is aptly named KnowSuccess because *you can't know success until you know yourself.*

AWARD FOR PRESENTATION EXCELLENCE. In 1997, Jeffrey was awarded the designation of Certified Speaking Professional (CSP) by the National Speakers Association. The CSP award has been given less than 500 times in the past 25 years and is the association's highest earned award.

BIG CORPORATE CUSTOMERS. Jeffrey's customers include Coca-Cola, D.R. Horton, Caterpillar, BMW, BNC Mortgage, Cingular Wireless, MacGregor Golf, Ferguson Enterprises, Kimpton Hotels, Hilton, Enterprise Rent-A-Car, AmeriPride, NCR, Stewart Title, Comcast Cable, Time Warner Cable, Liberty Mutual Insurance, Principal Financial Group, Wells Fargo Bank, Baptist Health Care, BlueCross BlueShield, Carlsberg Beer, Wausau Insurance, Northwestern Mutual, MetLife, The Sports Authority, GlaxoSmithKline, AC Neilsen, IBM, The New York Post, and hundreds of others.

Buy Gitomer, Inc.
310 Arlington Avenue Loft 329 • Charlotte, North Carolina 28203
office **704/333-1112** • *fax* **704/333-1011**
e-mail **jeffrey@gitomer.com** • *web* **www.gitomer.com**

Turn *The Little Green Book* Into Your GREEN

Jeffrey's *Little Green Book of Getting Your Way*
is available as a blended learning solution.

The Little Green Book of Getting Your Way
packaged training contains facilitator guides,
participant workbooks, multimedia support,
job aids, and e-learning reinforcement.

For more information
call 704-333-1112 and scream,

"I want my way!"

Other titles by Jeffrey Gitomer

THE LITTLE GOLD BOOK OF YES! ATTITUDE
(FT Press, 2007)

THE LITTLE BLACK BOOK OF CONNECTIONS
(Bard Press, 2006)

THE LITTLE RED BOOK OF SALES ANSWERS
(Pearson Prentice-Hall, 2006)

THE LITTLE RED BOOK OF SELLING
(Bard Press, 2004)

THE PATTERSON PRINCIPLES OF SELLING
(Lito Press, 2006)

CUSTOMER SATISFACTION IS WORTHLESS, CUSTOMER LOYALTY IS PRICELESS
(Bard Press, 1998)

THE SALES BIBLE
(HarperCollins, 1994)

"I've been listening to your motivational tapes while you're at work and I've decided to become a Great Dane!"